HOLT

Elements of
Language

Developmental
Language Skills

- Grammar
- Usage
- Mechanics

HOLT, RINEHART AND WINSTON

A Harcourt Education Company

Orlando • **Austin** • New York • San Diego • London

ISBN 978-0-03-099197-4
ISBN 0-03-099197-8

7 1186 15

4500544189

Contents

Contents

Using This Workbook

The worksheets in this workbook provide additional instruction, practice, and reinforcement for *Elements of Language* and for *Language Skills Practice*.

This workbook is designed to supplement *Language Skills Practice* by providing additional instruction and practice to students who have not yet mastered the rules and topics covered in *Elements of Language*.

You will find throughout the workbook several special features, which have been added to aid students' mastery of grammar, usage, and mechanics. The special features include notes, reminders, tips, points of instruction after instructional and exercise examples, and guided practice for the first one or two items in each exercise.

- **Notes** provide students with pertinent information related to the rule or topic covered on a given worksheet.

- **Reminders** review grammatical terms and concepts that were covered on previous worksheets.

- **Tips** provide students with tangible aids for understanding abstract concepts. These tips include mnemonic devices, identification tests, and recognition strategies.

- **Points of Instruction** explain how the rule or topic applies to the instructional and exercise examples provided.

- **Guided Practice** helps students with the first one or two items of each exercise by asking questions that guide students to the correct answer.

Teacher's Notes and an **Answer Key** are provided on the *Teacher One Stop*™ **DVD-ROM with ExamView® Test Generator**.

Symbols for Revising and Proofreading

Symbol	Example	Meaning of Symbol
≡	Fifty-first street	Capitalize a lowercase letter.
/	Jerry's Aunt	Lowercase a capital letter.
∧	differ^eant	Change a letter.
∧	The capital ^{of}Ohio	Insert a missing word, letter, or punctuation mark.
⌐	beside the ^{lake}river	Replace a word.
℘	Where's the the key?	Leave out a word, letter, or punctuation mark.
ℨ	an invisibile guest	Leave out and close up.
⌢	a close friend ship	Close up space.
∩	thier	Change the order of letters.
⟨tr⟩	Avoid having too many corrections of your paper in the final version.	Transfer the circled words. (Write *tr* in nearby margin.)
¶	¶"Hi," he smiled.	Begin a new paragraph.
⊙	Stay well	Add a period.
∧	Of course you may be wrong.	Add a comma.
#	icehockey	Add a space.
⊙	one of the following	Add a colon.
∧	Maria Simmons, M.D. Jim Fiorello, Ph.D.	Add a semicolon.
=	a great=grandmother	Add a hyphen.
∨	Pauls car	Add an apostrophe.
⟨stet⟩	On the fifteenth of July	Keep the crossed-out material. (Write *stet* in nearby margin.)

The Noun

Nouns

1a. A *noun* is a word or word group that is used to name a person, a place, a thing, or an idea.

PERSONS	Aunt Linda, teacher, co-pilot, athlete, Walter D. Myers
PLACES	stadium, Salt Lake City, football camp, Ireland, house
THINGS	saltshaker, horse, driveway, Big Dipper, jack-in-the-box
IDEAS	strength, happiness, Buddhism, amazement, self-confidence

TIP Try this test to decide whether a word is a noun. Place the word in the blank in one of the following sentences. If the word makes sense in the sentence, then the word is probably a noun.

EXAMPLES I need a new _____.   *or*   I admire _____.

I need a new <u>camera</u>.   I admire <u>creativity</u>.

Common and Proper Nouns

You may have noticed that some nouns begin with a lowercase letter while others are capitalized. A *common noun* names any one of a group of persons, places, things, or ideas and is generally not capitalized. A *proper noun* names a specific person, place, thing, or idea and is capitalized.

COMMON NOUNS friend, teenager, continent, dog, weekday, building

PROPER NOUNS Jordan Smith, Jamaal, Europe, Snoopy, Friday, Tower Bridge

EXERCISE A Underline each noun in the sentences below. Then, write *C* above the noun if it is a common noun, or *P* if it is a proper noun.

                     P   C   P

Example 1. <u>Victor</u> traveled across the <u>ocean</u> to <u>Africa</u>. [*Victor* names a specific person. *Ocean* names any one of a group of things. *Africa* names a specific place.]

1. Look at these photographs of my friend James, who is a relative of Victor. [Which words name any one of a group of persons or things? Which words name specific persons or things?]

2. Did the two men visit Madagascar, a large island near Africa?

3. Courage and curiosity are two qualities you will find in my friends.

4. Many different countries make up the large continent of Africa.

5. On his journey back to America, Victor sailed on the *Princess*.

GO ON

Compound Nouns

A *compound noun* is made up of two or more words used together as a single noun. Compound nouns might be written as one word, as separate words, or as a hyphenated word.

    ONE WORD   chairperson, hallway, basketball, spacecraft, oversight
    SEPARATE WORDS   Professor Johnson, mail carrier, Rhode Island, near miss
    HYPHENATED WORD   jack-of-all-trades, Austria-Hungary, sit-ups, self-respect

EXERCISE B Underline each noun in the following sentences. Then, if the noun is compound, write *CD* for *compound* above it.

Example 1. Lucy planted forget-me-nots in the flower bed. [*Lucy* names a person. *Forget-me-nots* and *bed* name things, and *forget-me-nots* is made up of more than one word.]

6. In gym class, Coach Ellis led the students through a set of twenty push-ups. [Which words name persons or things? Which nouns are made up of more than one word?]

7. After the children tossed snowballs, they built a snowman on the sidewalk.

8. Did Dad change the batteries in the smoke detector that is in the family room?

9. You should read *Homeless Bird* by Gloria Whelan, a winner of the National Book Award.

10. My sister-in-law, a singer in a band, also plays the guitar.

Collective Nouns

A *collective noun* is a word that names a group of people, animals, or things.

    COLLECTIVE NOUNS   audience, chorus, committee, flock, herd, batch, bundle, cluster

EXERCISE C Underline the collective noun in each of the following pairs of nouns.

Examples 1. batch   biscuits   [*Batch* names a group of things.]

    2. robins   flock   [*Flock* names a group of animals.]

11. collection   DVDs [Which word names a group of things?]

12. wolves   pack [Which word names a group of animals?]

13. gnats   swarm

14. family   children

15. players   team

16. employees   staff

17. squad   officers

18. council   advisors

19. whales   pod

20. Congress   senators

The Pronoun A

Pronouns

1b. A *pronoun* is a word that is used in place of one or more nouns or pronouns.

> **EXAMPLES** Andy called Mary. **He** invited **her** to a party. [*He* stands for *Andy. Her* stands for *Mary.*]
>
> Ruth sent invitations to Louis, Anna, and Ms. Pickett. **They** answered right away. [*They* stands for *Louis, Anna,* and *Ms. Pickett.*]

A pronoun stands for or refers to a word that is called the ***antecedent*** of the pronoun.

> **EXAMPLE** The **apple** lay beneath the tree where **it** had fallen. [The pronoun *it* stands for the noun *apple,* so *apple* is the antecedent of *it.*]

Personal Pronouns

A *personal pronoun* stands for the one speaking (first person), the one spoken to (second person), or the one spoken about (third person).

FIRST PERSON	I, me, my, mine, we, us, our, ours
SECOND PERSON	you, your, yours
THIRD PERSON	he, him, his, she, her, hers, it, its, they, them, their, theirs

> **EXAMPLE** **Your** kind words cheered **him.** [While the antecedents of the personal pronouns *Your* and *him* do not appear in the sentence, they are understood. *Your* stands for the one spoken to, and *him* stands for the one spoken about.]

EXERCISE A Underline each personal pronoun in the following sentences. Then, draw an arrow from the personal pronoun to its antecedent. Some sentences have more than one personal pronoun.

Example 1. Leo, your time may be the most valuable thing you can donate! [*Your* and *you* stand

for *Leo. Leo* is the antecedent of *your* and *you.*]

1. Many teens volunteer their time to worthy causes. [What noun does *their* stand for?]

2. Lonny volunteers at an animal shelter. He grooms the dogs.

3. Does Alfredo teach songs to the children at his church?

4. At the local hospital, Nina helps the nurses; she does simple chores for them.

5. Search the Internet for ideas. It lists volunteer programs in many cities.

GO ON ▶

EXERCISE B Write an appropriate personal pronoun on the blank in each of the following sentences.

Example 1. My mother and I found these quartz crystals. ___We___ discovered them in a riverbed

near our home. [*We* can stand for both antecedents, *mother* and *I*.]

6. Kim rehearsed _____ lines. [What personal pronoun can be used in place of *Kim*?]

7. When _____ gets windy, the weather almost seems to invite us to fly kites.

8. "Mira," he said, "this book must belong to you. It has _____ name on it."

9. Arthur wants to raise the seat of his bicycle. Can you lend _____ a wrench?

10. "_____ built this radio all by myself!" Marta piped up.

Reflexive and Intensive Pronouns

A *reflexive pronoun* stands for the subject of the sentence and is required in order for the sentence to make sense. An **intensive pronoun** stresses its antecedent and is not required in order for the sentence to make sense. Reflexive and intensive pronouns end with the suffix *–self* or *–selves*.

REFLEXIVE PRONOUN Teresa reminded **herself** to lock the door. [*Herself* stands for the subject *Teresa* and completes the meaning of the sentence.]

INTENSIVE PRONOUN Teresa **herself** locked the door. [*Herself* stresses *Teresa*. *Herself* is not required for the sentence to make sense.]

TIP To decide whether a pronoun is reflexive or intensive, rewrite the sentence and leave out the pronoun. If the sentence still makes sense, the pronoun is intensive.

EXAMPLES I **myself** fixed it. [*I fixed it* makes sense. *Myself* is an intensive pronoun.]
I fixed it by **myself.** [*I fixed it by* does not make sense. *Myself* is a reflexive pronoun.]

EXERCISE C Read the following sentences, and decide whether the underlined pronoun is reflexive or intensive. On the line provided, write *REF* if the pronoun is reflexive or *INT* if the pronoun is intensive.

Example __REF__ **1.** The campers warmed themselves at the campfire. [Without *themselves*, the

sentence does not make sense. Therefore, *themselves* is reflexive.]

_____**11.** You should treat yourself to a nap. [Does the sentence make sense without *yourself*?]

_____**12.** The principal herself made the final decision.

_____**13.** Did the puppy enjoy itself during the outing to the park?

_____**14.** After I finished the story, I found myself laughing out loud.

_____**15.** Uncle Eric himself planned the model train layout.

The Pronoun B
Demonstrative Pronouns

A *demonstrative pronoun* points out a person, a place, a thing, or an idea. The demonstrative pronouns are *this, that, these,* and *those.*

> **EXAMPLES** **Those** are the members of the choir. [*Those* points out *members.*]
>
> Are **these** the ones you wanted? [*These* points out *ones.*]

TIP Think of *demonstrative pronouns* as pronouns that point at something. Imagine pointing your finger at an object and saying, "*This* is the cereal I want," or "*That* is the fastest horse."

NOTE *This, that, these,* and *those* are used as adjectives as well as pronouns. When they describe nouns or pronouns, they are called *demonstrative adjectives.* When they point out and stand for nouns or pronouns, they are called *demonstrative pronouns.*

> **EXAMPLES** Her sketch is more colorful than **this.** [*This* stands for and points out a specific thing, so it is a demonstrative pronoun.]
>
> Her sketch is more colorful than **this** drawing. [*This* tells which *drawing*, so it is a demonstrative adjective.]

EXERCISE A Underline the demonstrative pronoun in each of the following sentences.

Examples 1. Those are my handmade birthday cards. [*Those* points out *cards.*]

2. He said he couldn't be certain about that. [*That* points at something not named in the sentence.]

1. These are my favorite books of all time. [Which word points out *books*?]

2. Is this a serious tale of grand adventure, or is it just a silly story? [Which word points out *tale*?]

3. You two should really take a look at these!

4. My skateboard rolls as smoothly as those used in professional competitions.

5. Of the entire football season, that was the most suspenseful game!

6. This set of math problems is a lot like those.

7. When will we finish painting that?

8. Of all of these, the third one sounds the most appealing.

9. That is the first time she's ever eaten a kiwi fruit.

10. Think of this as an opportunity to shine!

GO ON

Interrogative Pronouns

An *interrogative pronoun* introduces a question. The interrogative pronouns are *who, whom, which, what,* and *whose.*

> **EXAMPLES** **Whose** was the best book report? [*Whose* introduces a question.]
>
> **What** is the cafeteria serving for lunch? [*What* introduces a question.]

EXERCISE B Decide whether the underlined pronoun in each sentence is a demonstrative pronoun or an interrogative pronoun. Then, on the line provided, write *DEM* for *demonstrative pronoun* or *INT* for *interrogative pronoun.*

Example __INT__ **1.** To <u>whom</u> did you send the e-mail about Kelly's party? [*Whom* introduces a

question.]

_____ **11.** <u>Which</u> of those cartoons was chosen for the front page of the school newspaper? [Does

Which introduce a question, or does it point out something?]

_____ **12.** Is <u>this</u> the final game of the basketball season?

_____ **13.** The life jackets for the members of our group are <u>those</u>.

_____ **14.** <u>What</u> does the symbol on your ring mean?

_____ **15.** <u>Whom</u> would you elect as Student Principal for a week?

EXERCISE C For each blank in the following sentences, write an appropriate demonstrative pronoun or interrogative pronoun. Use a different pronoun for each sentence.

Example 1. From ___whom___ should we get today's assignment? [*Whom* is an interrogative

pronoun that fits this sentence.]

16. Excuse me, but how much do _____ cost? [Which indefinite pronoun fits this sentence?]

17. Help me pass _____ out to the rest of the club.

18. _____ of the two maps is most up-to-date?

19. Of all the fossils I've found, _____ is my favorite.

20. _____ is the most sensible plan?

Third Course

The Pronoun C
Relative Pronouns

A *relative pronoun* introduces a subordinate clause. A relative pronoun generally relates the descriptive information found within a subordinate clause to a noun or pronoun found in the main clause. The relative pronouns are *that, which, who, whom,* and *whose.*

EXAMPLES   Mario owns a Great Dane, **which** is a very large dog. [*Which* introduces the subordinate clause *which is a very large dog* and relates this descriptive information to *Great Dane.*]

Mario, **who** owns a Great Dane, lives next door. [*Who* introduces the subordinate clause *who owns a Great Dane* and relates this descriptive information to *Mario.*]

Mario, **whom** neighbors often see outside, has a large yard. [*Whom* introduces the subordinate clause *whom neighbors often see outside* and relates this descriptive information to *Mario.*]

The Great Dane **that** Mario owns is almost always with him. [*That* introduces the subordinate clause *that Mario owns* and relates this descriptive information to *Great Dane.*]

REMINDER A *subordinate clause* has a subject and a verb, but the clause cannot stand alone as a sentence. Information contained in a subordinate clause is generally less important than the information contained in a sentence's main clause. ***Which fell from the sky*** is a subordinate clause. *Ted found a meteorite,* ***which fell from the sky*** is a complete sentence.

EXERCISE A Underline the relative pronoun in each of the following sentences.

Examples 1. Do you enjoy stories that are about time travel? [*That* begins the subordinate clause *that are about time travel.*]

2. You may enjoy *The Time Machine,* which was written by H. G. Wells. [*Which* begins the subordinate clause *which was written by H. G. Wells.*]

1. Chen is reading *Animal Farm,* which is about power and betrayal. [Which word begins a subordinate clause?]

2. George Orwell, who wrote this fable, used animals as main characters. [Which word begins a subordinate clause?]

3. The plot is about farm animals that chase away their owners!

4. Try reading a book by J.R.R. Tolkien, an author whom many readers admire.

5. Bilbo Baggins, whom readers meet in *The Hobbit,* is the hero of this story.

GO ON

6. A hobbit is a creature whose life centers on family, food, and a good home.

7. In many classrooms, students read books that explore the dark side of human nature.

8. Have you read *Lord of the Flies,* which is about human nature?

9. A group of boys, whose airplane crashes, must survive on a lonely island.

10. What do you think of these boys, who become savage?

EXERCISE B Underline the relative pronoun in each of the following sentences. Then, draw an arrow from the relative pronoun to the word to which the relative pronoun relates.

Examples 1. Li's trumpet, which is silver, always sparkles in the sunlight. [*Which* begins the sub-ordinate clause *which is silver* and relates the information to *trumpet.*]

2. How often should I water the plants that are in the front room? [*That* begins the subordinate clause *that are in the front room* and relates the information to *plants.*]

11. The pep rally, which began at one o'clock, lasted almost two hours! [Which relative pronoun begins a subordinate clause? To which noun does the relative pronoun relate?]

12. When should we pick up the uniforms that Ms. Baraka ordered? [Which relative pronoun begins a subordinate clause? To which noun does the relative pronoun relate?]

13. Marie, whom the community greatly admires, planted four trees in a local park.

14. Try finding a puzzle piece that is shaped like an *H.*

15. Ernesto's brother, who enjoys good conversation, makes it a point to visit us once a day.

16. We saw a whooping crane, which is one of the rarest birds in North America!

17. That short story, which talks about the love of a grandmother for her grandson, is excellent.

18. Is Leroy, whom our customers love, going to get this month's bonus?

19. Julia constructed this model volcano from clay that she found in her own backyard.

20. The choir's leaders, who are looking for a new sound, have been listening to Caribbean music.

The Pronoun D

Indefinite Pronouns

Most pronouns refer to specific persons, places, things, or ideas. An *indefinite pronoun* refers to one or more persons, places, things, or ideas that may or may not be specifically named in a sentence. An indefinite pronoun does not refer to a specific person, place, thing, or idea.

COMMONLY USED INDEFINITE PRONOUNS

all	both	many	none	some
another	each	more	no one	somebody
any	either	most	nothing	something
anybody	everyone	much	one	such
anyone	everything	neither	other	
anything	few	nobody	several	

> **EXAMPLES** **Several** of the envelopes had rare postage stamps on them. [*Several* refers to things named in the sentence, *envelopes,* but it does not refer to specific envelopes.]
>
> **Somebody** bought the collection of rare stamps. [*Somebody* refers to a person who is not named in the sentence, and it does not refer to a specific person.]

NOTE▶ Even though indefinite pronouns may not refer to specific persons, places, things, or ideas, they are still used in the same ways as other pronouns. In a sentence, indefinite pronouns can appear as subjects, direct objects, indirect objects, predicate nominatives, or as objects of prepositions.

> **EXAMPLES** **Everyone** in the van knew the store's address. [*Everyone* is an indefinite pronoun used as the subject of the sentence.]
>
> Did the librarian gather **everyone** into reading circles? [The indefinite pronoun *everyone* is used as the direct object of the verb *did gather.*]
>
> Mr. Benson gave **everyone** paper swans. [The indefinite pronoun *everyone* is used as an indirect object explaining to whom the swans were given.]
>
> Is this **everyone**? [The indefinite pronoun *everyone* is used as a predicate nominative of the verb *Is.*]

EXERCISE A Underline the indefinite pronouns in the following sentences.

Examples 1. Each of the lazy days was truly enjoyable. [*Each* refers to things named in the sentence, *days,* but it does not refer to a specific day.]

2. We probably should examine both of the salamanders closely. [*Both* refers to things named in the sentence, *salamanders,* but it does not refer to a specific pair of salamanders.]

1. All of the hotel's staff members were very helpful. [Which word refers to persons who are not specifically named?]

GO ON ▶

2. Most of the activities, in Jack's opinion, would be fun. [Which word refers to a group of things that are not specifically named?]

3. Of everything available to guests, the shuffleboard court was our favorite spot.

4. We played softball with anyone who wanted to play.

5. Let's meet Jack and the others at the lake behind the hotel.

6. Some of the rocks along the shore are quite beautiful.

7. We could give somebody the prettiest stones.

8. Wouldn't Aunt Suzy want a few of them?

9. Save something to help you remember that trip!

10. I think we'd all gladly take another.

EXERCISE B For each blank in the following sentences, write an appropriate indefinite pronoun. Use a different indefinite pronoun for each sentence.

Examples 1. ____Many____ of my friends like baseball. [*Many* is one indefinite pronoun that makes sense in this sentence.]

   2. ____Neither____ of the two kittens has its eyes open. [*Neither* is one indefinite pronoun that makes sense in this sentence.]

11. _____ of the three computer games has its advantages. [Which indefinite pronoun would make sense in this sentence?]

12. Hans would like to own _____ of the watches. [Which indefinite pronoun would make sense in this sentence?]

13. Yes, please, I think I'll have _____ .

14. She said that she would love to talk with _____ who studies prairie dogs.

15. _____ of this essay is about how often chimpanzees behave like children.

16. I asked Nadine whether she had an extra pencil, and she said that she had _____ .

17. Mark said that he remembered absolutely _____ .

18. With a calm and reassuring smile, Warren greeted _____ .

19. The biologists built _____ a model cell.

20. Is _____ ready to talk about the space program?

Third Course

The Adjective

Adjectives

1c.   An *adjective* is a word that is used to modify a noun or a pronoun.

An adjective helps to define or describe a noun or pronoun by telling *what kind, which one,* or *how many* about that noun or pronoun.

> **WHAT KIND?**   **clean** room, **brown** hair, **French** pen pal, **easy** test
>
> **WHICH ONE?**   **first** choice, **that** calendar, **this** box, **next** class
>
> **HOW MANY?**   **many** fish, **six** songs, **some** ideas, **few** coins

NOTE *A, an,* and *the* are special adjectives that we call *articles. A* and *an* are ***indefinite articles*** because they refer to any member of a group. *The* is the ***definite article*** because it refers to a specific member of a group.

EXERCISE A Underline each adjective in the following sentences. Each sentence has more than one adjective. Do not underline the articles *a, an,* and *the.*

Example 1. Find a <u>safe</u> path around <u>those</u> <u>four</u> <u>huge</u> rocks. [*Safe* modifies *path. Those, four,* and *huge* modify *rocks.*]

1. There is a large family of healthy ducks by the lake. [Which word modifies *family*? Which word modifies *ducks*?]

2. During the hot afternoon, several deer crossed the grassy meadow.

3. Look at the small, brown rabbit near the trees.

4. A gray dove looked for tiny seeds beneath a leafy, green bush.

5. Did you see the beautiful fur on that fox?

Pronoun or Adjective?

Some words, such as *either, neither, which, this, these,* or *that,* may be used as either pronouns or adjectives. When these words take the place of nouns or other pronouns, they are pronouns. When they modify nouns or pronouns, they are adjectives.

> **PRONOUNS** I wore **this.**   She knows **neither.**   **Which** won?
>
> **ADJECTIVES** I wore **this** hat.   She knows **neither** boy.   **Which** team won?

NOTE When the ***demonstrative pronouns*** *this, that, these,* and *those* modify nouns or pronouns, they are called ***demonstrative adjectives.***

GO ON

Developmental Language Skills

EXERCISE B Underline each adjective in the following sentences. Then, draw an arrow from each adjective to the noun or pronoun it modifies. Do not underline the articles *a, an,* and *the.*

Example 1. That young vine is dangling from this tree. [*That* and *young* modify *vine. This* modifies *tree.*]

6. Either coach can train the new team. [Which two words modify nouns?]

7. Which long table will seat the hungry students?

8. Those three rosebushes won't bloom for many weeks.

9. Recent graduates helped several teachers purchase those.

10. We realized that neither frog had been making that unusual noise.

NOTE▶ Many words that can stand alone as nouns can also be used as adjectives. Adjectives formed from proper nouns are called *proper adjectives.*

NOUNS	stone	history	Maine
ADJECTIVES	**stone** fence	**history** lesson	**Maine** lobster

Adjectives in Sentences

An adjective usually comes before the noun or pronoun it modifies. However, sometimes the adjective follows the word it modifies, and occasionally a word or words may come between the adjective and the word it modifies.

EXAMPLE The bus, **large** and **yellow,** carried us to school. [*Large* and *yellow* both modify and follow *bus.*]

EXERCISE C Decide whether each of the underlined words in the following sentences is used as an adjective, a noun, or a pronoun. If the word is used as an adjective, write *ADJ* on the line provided. If the word is used as a noun, write *N* on the line provided. If the word is used as a pronoun, write *PRO* on the line provided.

Example __ADJ__ **1.** We ate lunch at the kitchen table. [*Kitchen* modifies *table.*]

_____**11.** Is this the homemade pickle relish? [Does *this* modify a noun, or does it refer to a noun?]

_____**12.** The relish in this jar is delicious!

_____**13.** The relish was made from California cucumbers.

_____**14.** This is the relish from California.

_____**15.** This sandwich, because it's dry and plain, needs relish.

The Verb A

Verbs

1d. A **verb** is a word that is used to express action or a state of being.

> **EXAMPLES** Maria **built** a sandcastle. [*Built* expresses Maria's action.]
>
> Maria **feels** happy. [*Feels* expresses Maria's state of being.]

Action Verbs

An *action verb* expresses physical or mental action.

> **EXAMPLES** Maria **waved** to Debbie. [physical action]
>
> Maria **knows** Debbie. [mental action]

REMINDER When you identify action verbs, remember to include any helping verbs. Common helping verbs include *is, can, does, have, might, was,* and *will.*

EXERCISE A Underline the action verbs in each of the following sentences. Some sentences have more than one action verb.

Examples 1. People have played with yo-yos for at least three thousand years. [*Have played* is an action verb and its helping verb; together, they express physical action.]

2. A sapodilla tree grows for more than twenty years before growers tap it for chicle, an ingredient in chewing gum. [*Grows* and *tap* are action verbs that express physical action.]

1. John Loudon McAdam designed roads without costly rock foundations. [Which word expresses mental action?]

2. The first self-propelled American land vehicle ran under steam power. [Which word expresses physical action?]

3. The Colorado River toad secretes poison that can paralyze its predators temporarily.

4. During thunderstorms, lightning bolts create gases that eventually fertilize the soil.

5. Alchemists never produced gold from lead, but they invented tools that chemists use today.

6. Do mice dream?

7. The tube-shaped leaves of some pitcher plants fill with rainwater and trap insects.

8. Suddenly, hundreds of grasshoppers leapt into the air.

9. When a bug is caught in the sticky hairs of a sundew's leaf, the leaf curls around it.

10. On the longest day of summer in the Antarctic Circle, the sun never sets.

Transitive and Intransitive Verbs

A *transitive verb* expresses action that is directed toward a person, place, or thing. The subject of a transitive verb performs the action of the verb. The object of a transitive verb receives the action of the verb.

        EXAMPLE When **did** Amy **meet** you? [Amy's action, *did meet*, is directed toward *you*.]

An *intransitive verb* expresses action that is not directed toward an object.

        EXAMPLE Amy **smiled** sweetly. [Amy's action, *smiled*, is not directed toward an object.]

NOTE A verb may be transitive in one sentence and intransitive in another.

      TRANSITIVE Hank **drove** the car. [Hank's action, *drove*, is directed toward the *car*.]

    INTRANSITIVE Hank **drove** slowly. [Hank's action, *drove*, is not directed toward an object.]

EXERCISE B Decide whether the underlined verb in each sentence is a transitive or intransitive verb. Then, on the line provided, write *TR* for *transitive verb* or *INT* for *intransitive verb*.

Examples ___TR___ **1.** Did Selma <u>memorize</u> her locker combination? [The action *Did memorize* is directed toward *combination*.]

     ___INT___ **2.** Selma always <u>chatters</u> quickly and good-naturedly. [The action *chatters* is not directed toward an object.]

_____**11.** Jason <u>reads</u> each day during study hall. [Is the action directed toward an object?]

_____**12.** Usually, Jason <u>reads</u> a book for English class. [Is the action directed toward an object?]

_____**13.** <u>Will</u> Jason <u>help</u> you with your homework?

_____**14.** You and he <u>can go</u> to the library on Saturday.

_____**15.** At the library, the two boys <u>study</u> quietly.

_____**16.** Jason suddenly <u>laughs</u> out loud.

_____**17.** "Walter Mitty <u>daydreams</u> all the time," he said.

_____**18.** "He just <u>heard</u> his car's engine."

_____**19.** "Now he thinks that he <u>is flying</u> a plane!"

_____**20.** The librarian coughed and <u>peered</u> over her glasses at the boys.

The Verb B

Verbs

1d.   A **verb** is a word that is used to express action or a state of being.

Linking Verbs

A *linking verb* expresses a state of being by linking its subject to a word or word group that renames or describes the subject. This word or word group is called a **subject complement**.

EXAMPLES   The speaker **is** Sharon. [The verb *is* links the subject complement *Sharon* to the subject *speaker*.]

The trumpeter **sounded** excited. [The verb *sounded* links the subject complement *excited* to the subject *trumpeter*.]

COMMONLY USED LINKING VERBS

be	shall be	should be
being	will be	would be
am	has been	can be
is	have been	could be
are	had been	should have been
was	shall have been	would have been
were	will have been	could have been

OTHER FREQUENTLY USED LINKING VERBS

appear	grow	seem	stay
become	look	smell	taste
feel	remain	sound	turn

EXERCISE A   Underline the linking verbs in each of the sentences below. Some sentences contain more than one linking verb.

Examples 1. The satellite <u>remained</u> brightly visible for almost thirty seconds! [The verb *remained* links the subject complement *visible* to the subject *satellite*.]

2. I <u>am</u> sure that the test tube <u>feels</u> warmer now. [The verb *am* links the subject complement *sure* to its subject *I*, and the verb *feels* links the subject complement *warmer* to its subject *test tube*.]

1. Cassie thought that the radishes tasted wonderful. [Which verb links the subject complement *wonderful* to its subject *radishes*?]

2. Sandals are usually a good, comfortable shoe for warm weather. [Which verb links the subject complements *good* and *comfortable* to their subject *Sandals*?]

GO ON

3. Is Janelle's poster the one with the piano full of flowers on it?

4. The cricket in my room seemed noisy last night.

5. Mel looks confident; maybe he should be the leader.

6. This paint job could have been perfect, but the paint dripped.

7. Sophia became the first of us to ask, "Were cars really that slow back then?"

8. That mockingbird certainly sounds carefree.

9. His grandmother was one of the first women to teach at a university.

10. The music stayed loud and festive, even when the band grew tired.

NOTE Many linking verbs can be used as action verbs as well.

LINKING VERB Yoko **stayed** warm near the fire. [*Stayed* links *Yoko* with *warm*.]

ACTION VERB Yoko **stayed** near the fire. [*Stayed* expresses Yoko's action.]

EXERCISE B Decide whether the underlined verb in each sentence below is an action verb or a linking verb. On the line provided, write *A* for *action verb* or *L* for *linking verb*. Then, if the verb is a linking verb, circle the words that are linked by the verb.

Examples __L__ **1.** The old (house) always had looked slightly (spooky). [*Had looked* links *house* to *spooky*.]

__A__ **2.** Lisa had looked at it many times. [*Had looked* expresses Lisa's actions.]

_____**11.** Over the years, the lock had become rusty. [Does *had become* link its subject to an adjective, or does it express an action?]

_____**12.** With great difficulty, Lisa turned the key in the lock. [Does *turned* link its subject to a noun, or does it express an action?]

_____**13.** Inside, the empty house seemed perfectly silent.

_____**14.** Long ago, the dusty air had turned stale.

_____**15.** Lisa remained calm in spite of the eerie atmosphere.

_____**16.** Then she stood on the porch and felt better.

_____**17.** She could smell fresh-cut hay in the breeze.

_____**18.** Crops grew in the fields across the street from the house.

_____**19.** With a new coat of paint, it might be a nice place to live.

_____**20.** The house suddenly appeared far less spooky.

The Verb C

Verbs

1d. A **verb** is a word that is used to express action or a state of being.

> **EXAMPLES** Yesterday Paula **wrote** a song. [*Wrote* expresses action.]
>
> She **felt** lonely. [*Felt* expresses a state of being.]

Verb Phrases: Main Verbs and Helping Verbs

A *verb phrase* contains at least one main verb and one or more helping verbs. A helping verb helps the main verb express action or state of being.

The helping verbs include all forms of the verb *be*. The *be* verbs include *am, is, are, was, were, be, being,* and *been*. Other helping verbs include *can, could, did, do, does, had, has, have, may, might, must, shall, should, will,* and *would*.

> **VERB PHRASES** **was** laughing [The helping verb *was* helps the main verb *laughing*.]
>
> **must** remember [The helping verb *must* helps the main verb *remember*.]
>
> **may have** arrived [The helping verb *may have* helps the main verb *arrived*.]

NOTE Sometimes the parts of a verb phrase are separated by other words in the sentence.

> **EXAMPLES** **Was** Alexa **laughing** at my joke? [*Alexa* interrupts *Was* and *laughing*.]
>
> The guests **may have** already **arrived.** [*Already* interrupts *may have* and *arrived*.]

EXERCISE A Draw a line under the verb phrase in each of the following sentences. Then, draw a second line under each helping verb.

Examples 1. All of us <u>have been</u> happy with Paul's meals and desserts. [*Have* helps *been* express our state of being.]

2. <u>Will</u> Paul <u>be making</u> a pumpkin pie for dessert? [*Will* and *be* help *making* express Paul's future action.]

1. Pumpkins are known for their soft orange pulp and high water content. [Which word helps the main verb *known*?]

2. You may have eaten delicious pumpkin bread or pumpkin muffins. [Which words help the main verb *eaten*?]

3. That pumpkin was grown in Margaret's own backyard garden.

4. It had become ripe for harvest a few days ago.

5. The tough orange rind must be removed from the pumpkin.

6. Then, the orange pulp can be used for food.

7. We can save some of the seeds for next year's crop.

8. Should we toast the rest of the pumpkinseeds?

9. During late October, many people will carve a pumpkin.

10. Pumpkins have also been grown as food for livestock.

NOTE▶ The word _not_ is an adverb, and so is the contraction _n't. Not_ and _n't_ are never part of the verb phrase.

    EXAMPLES Chen **was** not **laughing** at my joke. [The verb phrase is _was laughing._]

                Edward **was**n't **laughing** at my joke. [The verb phrase is _was laughing._]

EXERCISE B Draw a line under the verb phrase in each of the following sentences. Then, draw a second line under each helping verb. Remember that _not_ and _n't_ are not part of the verb phrase.

Examples 1. The skating couldn't have been more enjoyable! [_Could_ and _have_ are helping verbs

        that help _been_ express a state of being. _N't_ is not part of the verb phrase.]

    2. Did eager fans completely fill the available seats? [_Did_ is a helping verb that helps _fill_

        express action.]

11. Do you enjoy ice-skating and other winter sports? [Which words express action?]

12. Diego and I have often watched skating competitions on television. [Which words express

action?]

13. I myself have never worn a pair of ice skates.

14. My sister, however, will frequently compete in skating matches.

15. The coldness of the icy arena doesn't bother her.

16. Since childhood, she has always enjoyed the competitive nature of sports.

17. You should not have missed the competition last week.

18. Will you attend the match on Saturday afternoon?

19. We have always sat in one of the front rows.

20. We will not miss a single bit of action from those great seats.

                    Third Course

The Adverb

Adverbs

1e. An *adverb* modifies a verb, an adjective, or another adverb.

An adverb makes the meaning of the verb, adjective, or adverb more definite by telling *where, when, how,* or *to what extent.*

Adverbs Modifying Verbs

Adverbs modify verbs and also may introduce questions. Adverbs may come before or after the verbs they modify. Adverbs may also come between verbs in a verb phrase.

> **EXAMPLES**   Write his name **here.** [*Here* tells where to write his name.]
>
> She will **politely** ask. [*Politely* tells how she will ask.]
>
> **When** did Adam call you? [*When* introduces a question.]

NOTE Some words that can be used as nouns can also be used as adverbs.

> **NOUN**   **Today** is my birthday. [*Today* is the subject and is a noun.]
>
> **ADVERB**   **Today** I am celebrating my birthday. [*Today* tells when I *am celebrating* my birthday and is an adverb.]

EXERCISE A Underline the adverb in each of the following sentences. Then, draw an arrow from the adverb to the word or words it modifies.

Example 1. When did you buy the new telephone? [*When* modifies *did buy* by telling when.]

1. Please write your new phone number there. [Which word tells where about the verb?]

2. Loudly, the telephone in Becca's room rang.

3. Where did she earn the money for her own phone?

4. Becca mows lawns weekly for extra money.

5. She had carefully saved money for the phone.

Adverbs Modifying Adjectives

Adverbs also modify adjectives.

> **EXAMPLES**   **Extremely** spicy tacos were served. [*Extremely* modifies *spicy,* telling to what extent.]
>
> That story was **creatively** brilliant! [*Creatively* modifies *brilliant,* telling how.]

GO ON

EXERCISE B Underline the adverb in each of the sentences below. Then, draw an arrow from the adverb to the adjective it modifies.

Example 1. The pink blossoms on this rose bush are <u>fully</u> open. [*Fully* modifies *open.*]

6. Whose incredibly delicious casserole is this? [Which word modifies an adjective?]

7. Rather large trees surround the car lot.

8. After a long afternoon, I can say that my chores are nearly complete.

9. An especially valuable player receives the MVP award.

10. Please give a snack to the children, who are slightly hungry.

Adverbs Modifying Other Adverbs

Adverbs also modify other adverbs.

> **EXAMPLES** Heather plays volleyball **really** well. [*Really* modifies *well*, telling to what extent.]
>
> She **almost** never misses a serve. [*Almost* modifies *never*, telling to what extent.]

EXERCISE C Underline the adverb that modifies another adverb in each of the sentences below. Then, draw an arrow from the adverb to the adverb it modifies. Do not underline any adverbs that modify verbs or adjectives.

Example 1. Janis swims in the lake <u>only</u> rarely. [*Only* modifies *rarely* and tells to what extent.]

11. Why is he speaking very quietly? [Which word modifies an adverb?]

12. Somewhat excitedly, the child accepted the gift.

13. Both students completed the test equally quickly.

14. A fire broke out, but firefighters arrived quite soon.

15. You interpreted the poem extremely creatively.

The Preposition

1f. A *preposition* is a word that shows the relationship of a noun or pronoun to another word.

> **EXAMPLES** An insect **under** the table buzzed. [*Under* shows the relationship of *table* to *insect*.]
>
> An insect flew **near** my head. [*Near* shows the relationship of *head* to *flew*.]

COMMONLY USED PREPOSITIONS

about	before	down	in	of	since
above	behind	during	inside	off	through
across	beside	except	into	onto	toward
after	between	for	like	outside	until
at	by	from	near	over	without

The noun or pronoun that the preposition relates another word to is called the **object of the preposition.**

> **EXAMPLES** An insect behind the **table** buzzed. [*Table* is the noun that the preposition *behind* relates to *insect*. *Table* is the object of the preposition *behind*.]
>
> An insect above **it** buzzed. [*It* is the pronoun that the preposition *above* relates to *insect*. *It* is the object of the preposition *above*.]

Prepositions that are made of two or more words are called **compound prepositions.** Some compound prepositions are *according to, aside from, because of, in addition to, in front of, in place of, next to,* and *on account of.*

> **EXAMPLES** We were late **because of** heavy traffic.
>
> May I borrow the book **next to** your elbow?

EXERCISE A Underline the preposition in each of the following sentences. Then, draw two lines under the object of the preposition. Remember to underline all words in a compound preposition.

Example 1. According to the schedule, we will take a break now. [*Schedule* is the object of the compound preposition *According to.*]

1. Everyone was frightened during the scary movie. [Which word is a preposition? Which noun is the object of the preposition?]

2. Without a hat, Ellen's hair always lightens.

3. Jeff, you can use chicken in place of the beef.

4. The beautiful full moon disappeared behind thick clouds.

5. How can I choose between two good choices?

GO ON

The object of a preposition may be compound.

> **EXAMPLES** We talked **about nutrition** and **exercise.** [Both *nutrition* and *exercise* are objects of the preposition *about*.]
>
> This gift is **from Leon** and **Betty.** [Both *Leon* and *Betty* are objects of the preposition *from*.]

A *prepositional phrase* consists of the preposition, its object, and any modifiers of the object. The modifiers of the object can come before or after the object.

> **EXAMPLES** Marcos is going **to a new school.** [*School* is the object of the preposition *to*. *School* is modified by *a* and *new*.]
>
> Marcos is going **to the school that just opened.** [*School* is the object of the preposition *to*. *School* is modified by *the* and by the clause *that just opened*.]

NOTE▶ The word *to* can start both a prepositional phrase (*to the park*) and an infinitive phrase (*to run*). If *to* is followed by a verb, then the phrase is infinitive and not prepositional.

EXERCISE B Underline the preposition in each of the following sentences. Then, draw two lines under the object of the preposition. Remember to underline all words in a compound object. Each sentence has more than one prepositional phrase.

Examples 1. In the photograph, I am standing next to him and Pamela. [*Photograph* is the object of the preposition *In*. *Him* and *Pamela* are the objects of the preposition *next to*.]

2. When should we get on the ferry that's taking us over the bay? [*Ferry* is the object of the preposition *on*. *Bay* is the object of the preposition *over*.]

6. Because of the fire, smoke billowed from the windows and doors. [Which word is the object of a compound preposition? Which words are compound objects of a preposition?]

7. Since last Monday, I have been leaving the house before you each morning. [Which words are prepositions? Which words are objects of prepositions?]

8. The story is about a horse that gallops next to bicyclists.

9. Aside from a few loose boards, the bridge across the stream looks safe.

10. Look at the perfect blanket of snow on the streets and lawns.

11. Felicia skipped through the open gate in front of her house.

12. In addition to old newspapers, Toni collects cans during recycling drives.

13. Couldn't we use the tomatoes we grew instead of those from a store?

14. Since he got to sit behind the dugout, Cedric stayed through the final inning.

15. Should we climb aboard the boat beside the dock?

for **CHAPTER 1: PARTS OF SPEECH OVERVIEW**   `pages 77–80`

The Conjunction and the Interjection

The Conjunction

1g.   A *conjunction* is a word that joins words or word groups.

A *coordinating conjunction* joins words or word groups that are used in the same way. The coordinating conjunctions are *and, but, or, nor, for, yet*, and *so*.

> **EXAMPLES**   Roland bought juice **and** milk. [*And* joins two nouns, *juice* and *milk*.]
>
> Is the juice inside the refrigerator **or** on the counter? [*Or* joins two prepositional phrases, *inside the refrigerator* and *on the counter*.]
>
> Roland was thirsty, **so** he drank some juice. [*So* joins two independent clauses, *Roland was thirsty* and *he drank some juice*.]

A *correlative conjunction* is a pair of conjunctions that join words or word groups that are used in the same way. The correlative conjunctions are *both . . . and, not only . . . but also, either . . . or, neither . . . nor*, and *whether . . . or*.

> **EXAMPLES**   Roland bought **both** juice **and** milk. [*Both . . . and* joins two nouns, *juice* and *milk*.]
>
> The juice is **either** inside the refrigerator **or** on the counter. [*Either . . . or* joins two prepositional phrases, *inside the refrigerator* and *on the counter*.]
>
> **Not only** was Roland thirsty, **but** he was **also** hungry. [*Not only . . . but also* joins two independent clauses, *was Roland thirsty* and *he was hungry*.]

EXERCISE A Identify the conjunctions in the following sentences. Draw one line under coordinating conjunctions and two lines under correlative conjunctions.

Examples 1. I didn't know <u><u>whether</u></u> I should laugh <u><u>or</u></u> I should cry. [*Whether . . . or* joins two independent clauses, *I should laugh* and *I should cry*.]

        2. According to Meg, the judge's decision was strict <u>but</u> fair. [*But* joins two adjectives, *strict* and *fair*.]

1. I had met the girl before, yet I couldn't remember her name. [Which word joins two independent clauses?]

2. We heard the fire alarm not only in the hallways but also in the classrooms. [Which words join two prepositional phrases?]

3. After the assembly, I couldn't find Mark or Chi anywhere.

4. Do you know whether Carlos sanded or painted the bookcase?

5. On the beach and in the water, the family played happily.

6. Mr. Paulson had expected neither the award nor the party.

7. Was either the principal or the vice-principal present at the ceremony?

8. I will enjoy the winter break, but I will miss my friends.

9. Will this bus take us to both the mall and the library?

10. Neither the computer nor the printer was turned on.

The Interjection

1h. | An *interjection* is a word that expresses emotion. An interjection has no grammatical relation to the rest of the sentence.

Commonly used interjections include *ah, hey, oh, ouch, well, wow,* and *yippee.*

NOTE▶ Because an interjection does not serve a grammatical function in the sentence, it is set off from the sentence by an exclamation point, a comma, or commas.

> **EXAMPLES**   **Uh-oh!** I lost my watch.
>
> **Well,** I'm not sure where your watch is.
>
> A new one will cost, **oh,** about ten dollars.

EXERCISE B Identify the underlined word or group of words in each sentence. On the line provided, write *CRD* for *coordinating conjunction, CORR* for *correlative conjunction,* or *INT* for *interjection.*

Examples ___INT___ **1.** I was digging in the garden when, <u>yikes</u>, I saw a garter snake. [*Yikes* expresses emotion. It has no grammatical function in the sentence.]

___CORR___ **2.** I <u>not only</u> was digging in the garden <u>but also</u> was planting vegetables. [*Not only ... but also* is a correlative conjunction that joins two verb phrases.]

_____ **11.** Dad really likes carrots, <u>so</u> I will plant a lot of them. [Does the underlined word join two word groups, or does it express emotion?]

_____ **12.** <u>Ouch</u>! Did you know that blackberry vines have thorns on them? [Does the underlined word join two words, or does it express emotion?]

_____ **13.** <u>Either</u> the wild rabbits <u>or</u> the squirrels have nibbled on the strawberries.

_____ **14.** I planted several kinds of seeds, <u>yet</u> not all of them have sprouted.

_____ **15.** In that patch I planted, <u>ah</u>, lettuce.

_____ **16.** <u>Whoa</u>! Watch where you step in the garden!

_____ **17.** Shall we plant <u>both</u> vegetables <u>and</u> flowers in this garden?

_____ **18.** After an hour's work, we had finally pulled all the weeds. <u>Whew</u>!

_____ **19.** Should we place the scarecrow between the rows <u>or</u> in the corner?

_____ **20.** There is enough squash <u>not only</u> for our family <u>but also</u> for the neighbors.

The Subject
The Complete Subject

Every sentence contains a *subject* and a *predicate*.

2b. The **subject** tells whom or what the sentence is about, and the **predicate** says something about the subject.

The *complete subject* consists of the simple subject and any words, phrases, or clauses that modify the simple subject.

> **EXAMPLES** **The bells in the tower** rang loudly. [What rang loudly? The bells in the tower did. *The bells in the tower* is the complete subject.]
>
> Every morning, **the loud cry of my neighbors' rooster** wakes me. [What wakes me? The loud cry of my neighbors' rooster does. *The loud cry of my neighbors' rooster* is the complete subject.]

EXERCISE A Underline the complete subject in each of the following sentences.

Example 1. Did <u>Janet's older sister</u> compete at the track meet? [Who competed at the track meet?

Janet's older sister did. *Janet's older sister* is the complete subject.]

1. The light above the sink went out yesterday. [What went out yesterday?]

2. The biology students collected different types of leaves.

3. Did Dad enjoy the baseball game?

4. The purple and blue flowers really brightened up the room.

5. When will the band members return from the field trip?

The Simple Subject

2c. The main word or word group that tells whom or what the sentence is about is called the **simple subject.**

> **EXAMPLES** The **bells** in the tower rang loudly. [What rang loudly? Bells did. *Bells* is the simple subject.]
>
> Where will **you** hang the new painting? [Who will hang the painting? You will. *You* is the simple subject.]

TIP The simple subject is never found in a prepositional phrase. A **preposition** is a word that tells the relationship of a noun or pronoun to another word in the sentence. Some common prepositions are *about, among, at, for, from, in, of, under,* and *with*. To find the simple subject, cross out any preposition and the noun or pronoun that follows it.

> **EXAMPLE** The **bells** ~~in the tower~~ rang loudly. [*Bells* is the subject, not *tower*.]

GO ON

Sometimes the simple subject is also the complete subject.

> **EXAMPLE** **Nina** volunteers at the humane society. [*Nina* is both the simple subject and the complete subject.]

EXERCISE B Underline the complete subject once and the simple subject twice in each of the following sentences.

Example 1. Is your history class studying the ancient world? [Who is studying? Your history class is. *Your history class* is the complete subject. *Class* is the simple subject.]

6. The great pyramids of Egypt have become famous. [What have become famous?]

7. They were used as royal burial chambers.

8. Have you ever seen a pyramid?

9. Many different cultures built pyramids.

10. Examples of these unique structures can be found in Egypt and Mexico.

Compound Subjects

2f. A *compound subject* consists of two or more subjects that are joined by a conjunction and that have the same verb.

A compound subject consists of two or more words. Conjunctions commonly used to join the words of a compound subject are *and, or, neither . . . nor,* and *not only . . . but also.*

> **EXAMPLES** **Doug** and **Eddy** shoveled snow. [*Doug* and *Eddy* are parts of the compound subject joined by *and*. They have the same verb, *shoveled*.]
> Neither **Paul** nor **Ruth** wanted to see a movie after dinner. [*Paul* and *Ruth* are parts of the compound subject joined by *Neither . . . nor*. They have the same verb, *wanted*.]

EXERCISE C Underline the simple subject in each of the following sentences. Remember to underline each word in a compound subject.

Example 1. Does Nevada or Utah border California? [What borders California? Nevada or Utah does. *Nevada* and *Utah* are parts of the compound subject joined by *or*.]

11. Turtles and bullfrogs lived at the edge of the lake. [What lived at the edge of the lake?]

12. Neither onions nor peppers were in the stew.

13. Did Rosa, Barbara, and Fredric work together on the experiment?

14. Not only the cows but also the chickens must be fed.

15. Sally or Eugene will give a speech today.

The Predicate

The Simple Predicate

Every sentence contains a *subject* and a *predicate*.

2d. The *simple predicate,* or *verb,* is the main word or word group that tells something about the subject.

> **EXAMPLE** Matt **spoke** about his vacation to the Grand Canyon. [*Spoke* is the simple predicate and tells what Matt did.]

REMINDER▶ A simple predicate can be a one-word verb or a verb phrase.

> **EXAMPLES** Sally carefully **jumped** over the puddle. [The verb *jumped* tells what Sally did.]
>
> **Did** Sally **jump** over the puddle? [The verb phrase is *Did jump.* The words in the verb phrase are separated by the subject, *Sally,* and tell what Sally did.]

EXERCISE A Underline the simple predicate in each of the following sentences. Be sure to underline all words in a verb phrase.

Example 1. Karen and Paul <u>were talking</u> about computers. [The simple predicate *were talking* tells what Karen and Paul were doing.]

1. Cedric and Melissa drank water during the long, hot afternoon. [What did Cedric and Melissa do?]

2. We will practice on the soccer field today.

3. You should show Ms. Drake a copy of your short story.

4. The snowy mountain peaks shone in the morning sun.

5. Someone must have found the wallet in the park.

The Complete Predicate

The *complete predicate* consists of a verb and all the words that describe the verb and complete its meaning.

> **EXAMPLE** Jason **was attentively listening to the radio.** [The simple predicate is *was listening.* The complete predicate is *was attentively listening to the radio.*]

Sometimes the simple predicate is also the complete predicate.

> **EXAMPLE** The plane **is landing.** [*Is landing* is the simple predicate and the complete predicate.]

GO ON ▶

NOTE▶ The predicate usually comes after the subject. Sometimes, however, part or all of the predicate comes before the subject.

> **EXAMPLES**   **Yesterday** Bonnie **took her dog to the veterinarian.** [Part of the complete predicate comes before the subject.]
>
> **Perching on the edge of the cliff was** a hawk. [All of the complete predicate comes before the subject.]

EXERCISE B Underline the complete predicate once and the simple predicate twice in each of the following sentences.

Example 1. Mary is donating her old stuffed animals to the children's shelter. [The complete

predicate tells what Mary is doing. The simple predicate is *is donating*.]

6. The basketball team will be playing in the semifinals. [What will the basketball team do?]

7. Does your aunt own the nursery on Park Street?

8. In the shade of the oak tree, grass does not grow.

9. Calvin has been taking piano lessons for five years.

10. The kittens are playing.

The Compound Verb

2g.   A ***compound verb*** consists of two or more verbs that are joined by a conjunction and that have the same subject.

> **EXAMPLE**   The freshmen **yelled** the loudest at the pep rally and **won** the spirit award. [The compound verb is *yelled* and *won*. Both *yelled* and *won* tell about the same subject, *freshmen*. The parts of the compound verb are joined by the conjunction *and*.]

EXERCISE C Underline the simple predicate in each of the following sentences. Be sure to underline each part of a compound verb and all parts of a verb phrase.

Example 1. Does Josie's little brother follow her and imitate her actions? [The simple predicate is

the compound verb *Does follow* and *imitate*.]

11. Both tennis players inspected their rackets and practiced their swings. [What did both tennis

players do?]

12. Would you run the cash register or wrap purchases for me?

13. The bird had collected bits of straw and made a nest.

14. High above the crowd, the trapeze artists swung and leaped gracefully.

15. In the afternoon, my dogs sit on the patio and wait for me.

Predicate Nominatives

2i(1). A *predicate nominative* is a word or word group that is in the predicate and that identifies the subject or refers to it.

A predicate nominative appears only in a sentence that has a linking verb. Common linking verbs include *is, was, will be, has been,* and *could have been.*

EXAMPLES

              S   V   PN

My costume for the play is an old **tuxedo.** [The noun *tuxedo* identifies the subject, *costume.*]

       V   S   V   PN

Could the winner of the poetry contest have been **she?** [The pronoun *she* identifies the subject, *winner.*]

     S   V   PN

One of the winners must be **Keith Bryant.** [The word group *Keith Bryant* identifies the subject, *One.*]

EXERCISE A Underline the predicate nominative in each of the following sentences.

Example 1. The campers with the large, blue tent are <u>they</u>. [The pronoun *they* identifies the subject, *campers. They* is the predicate nominative.]

1. Amber's new pet is a goldfish. [Which word identifies the subject, *pet*?]

2. Each Saturday, the umpire has been Mr. Nelson.

3. Ms. Higdon is my art teacher.

4. The secret herbs for the sauce are these.

5. For the last thirty years, my grandfather has been a farmer.

TIP To find the predicate nominative in a question, turn the question into a statement.

     QUESTION Was that beautiful bouquet of flowers a gift?

                             S   V   PN

    STATEMENT That beautiful bouquet of flowers was a gift. [The word order of the statement makes it easier to tell that *gift* is the predicate nominative.]

EXERCISE B Underline the predicate nominative in each of the following sentences.

Examples 1. Is the president of the student council <u>Chen Tran</u>? [*Chen Tran* identifies the subject, *president. Chen Tran* is the predicate nominative.]

2. That grandfather clock is an <u>antique</u>. [*Antique* identifies the subject, *grandfather clock. Antique* is the predicate nominative.]

6. The building on the corner is city hall. [Which word group identifies the subject, *building*?]

GO ON

7. How long has Aunt Rosa been a dance instructor? [Which word identifies the subject, *Aunt Rosa*?]

8. Is your uncle an architect?

9. My favorite poet is William Carlos Williams.

10. Was the person sitting on the steps she?

11. The people in yellow shirts are volunteers.

12. Is your mother a member of the PTA?

13. She has been my best friend since third grade.

14. Car washes are usually good fund-raisers.

15. Are those flowers bluebonnets?

A linking verb can have more than one predicate nominative. Two or more predicate nominatives of the same linking verb are called a *compound predicate nominative.*

 V   S   V   PN   PN   PN

EXAMPLE Over the years, has Uncle Danny been a **cyclist,** a **runner,** and a **golfer?**
[*Cyclist, runner,* and *golfer* identify the subject, *Uncle Danny.* Together, *cyclist, runner,* and *golfer* make up the compound predicate nominative.]

EXERCISE C Underline the predicate nominative in each of the following sentences. Remember to underline all parts of a compound predicate nominative.

Examples 1. My heroes are firefighters and police officers. [*Firefighters* and *police officers* identify the subject, *heroes.*]

      2. Is *Mozart* your final answer? [*Answer* identifies the subject, *Mozart.*]

16. The winners of the contest were Sally Chavez and Fred Browning. [Which word groups identify the subject, *winners*?]

17. My brother Terrell is an accountant and a little league coach. [Which words identify the subject, *Terrell*?]

18. Will you be a judge for the costume contest?

19. My favorite pieces of clothing are these pants and that sweater.

20. This strange sea creature must be a sea horse.

21. The people at the door were my aunt, uncle, and cousins.

22. The lost treasure was jewels and gold coins.

23. Are the nominees for teacher of the year Ms. Ferguson, Mr. Price, and Mrs. Martinez?

24. Is she a contestant or a judge?

25. The next performer should be she.

Third Course

Predicate Adjectives

2i(2). A **predicate adjective** is an adjective that is in the predicate and that modifies the subject.

Predicate adjectives complete the meaning of linking verbs and describe the subject. Predicate adjectives follow linking verbs such as *is, are, will be, has been, appear, feel, grow, look, smell, sound,* and *taste.*

EXAMPLES Margaret was very **tired** after the swim meet. [The adjective *tired* describes the subject, *Margaret*, and completes the meaning of the linking verb *was*. Therefore, *tired* is the predicate adjective.]

Doesn't this orange look **juicy**? [The adjective *juicy* describes the subject, *orange*, and completes the meaning of the linking verb *Does look*. Therefore, *juicy* is the predicate adjective.]

REMINDER An adjective is a word that describes a person, place, thing, or idea. An adjective usually answers the question *what kind? how many?* or *which one?*

EXERCISE A Underline the predicate adjective in each of the following sentences.

Examples 1. Does the song on the radio sound <u>familiar</u>? [*Familiar* describes the subject, *song. Familiar* is the predicate adjective.]

      2. My niece is quite <u>musical</u>. [*Musical* describes the subject, *niece. Musical* is the predicate adjective.]

1. The high school's football field was muddy. [Which word in the predicate describes the subject, *field?*]

2. In her wedding gown, my sister looked quite beautiful. [Which word in the predicate describes the subject, *sister?*]

3. Do the potatoes taste too salty?

4. Finally, the floors in the hallways were clean.

5. Is the new student friendly?

6. This article about the elephants is interesting.

7. Kim's costume was very creative.

8. After the car wash, Manuel felt exhausted.

9. Wow! Your locker is extremely organized.

10. Without the lights on, this room looks gloomy.

GO ON

Compound Predicate Adjectives

A linking verb can have more than one predicate adjective. Two or more predicate adjectives that describe the same subject are called a *compound predicate adjective.*

> **EXAMPLES** How **tired** and **sleepy** I am! [*Tired* and *sleepy* both describe the subject, *I.*]
>
> Are these drums too **loud** or too **quiet**? [*Loud* and *quiet* both describe the subject, *drums.*]
>
> The scientist is **talented, creative,** and **young.** [*Talented, creative,* and *young* describe the subject, *scientist.*]

EXERCISE B Underline the predicate adjectives in the following sentences. Remember to underline all parts of a compound predicate adjective.

Examples 1. How <u>long</u> should my article for the newspaper be? [*Long* describes the subject, *article.*]

2. My aunt is <u>kind</u> and <u>considerate</u>. [*Kind* and *considerate* describe the subject, *aunt.*]

11. This book was incredibly interesting and suspenseful. [Which words in the predicate describe the subject, *book?*]

12. Was the family reunion enjoyable or boring? [Which words in the predicate describe the subject, *reunion?*]

13. During the basketball game your moves were fantastic!

14. Was Brett happy about the decision?

15. The express train seems modern, speedy, and reliable.

16. Does the fruit punch taste too sweet?

17. Your new friend appears shy yet friendly.

18. After completing the ten kilometer race, my grandfather was thirsty.

19. Was my presentation too long?

20. All afternoon the puppies have been energetic, playful, and entertaining.

Direct Objects

2j. A *direct object* is a noun, pronoun, or word group that tells who or what receives the action of a verb or shows the result of the action.

Direct objects complete the meaning of action verbs. They answer *Whom?* or *What?* after the verb.

                              V   **DO**

EXAMPLES Luisa played the **guitar.** [Played what? Played guitar. *Guitar* is the direct object.]

                            V   **DO**

Mel heard **her.** [Heard whom? Heard her. *Her* is the direct object.]

                           V   **DO**

Toni Morrison won the **Nobel Prize for Literature** in 1993. [Won what? Won the Nobel Prize for Literature. *Nobel Prize for Literature* is the direct object.]

EXERCISE A Underline the direct object in each of the following sentences.

Examples 1. Did the art students visit a <u>museum</u>? [Did visit what? Did visit a museum. *Museum* is the direct object.]

      2. I watered the <u>plants</u> on the patio. [Watered what? Watered plants. *Plants* is the direct object.]

1. Do you admire Abraham Lincoln? [Which word group answers the question *Whom do you admire?*]

2. After the competition, Coach Rogers posted the scores. [Which word answers the question *What did Coach Rogers post?*]

3. The squirrels collected acorns for the winter.

4. Pay the cashier at the entrance.

5. Has Martha ever seen *The Wizard of Oz*?

6. The dogs chased the rabbit across the field.

7. We all rode our bikes to the park.

8. Did you meet Michelle?

9. Each week, we recycle our aluminum cans.

10. The mountain overshadowed the village.

GO ON

Compound Direct Objects

An action verb may have more than one direct object. Two or more direct objects that complete the meaning of the same verb are called a *compound direct object.*

V   DO   DO

EXAMPLE Chen draws **cars** and **motorcycles.** [Draws what? Draws cars and motorcycles. *Cars* and *motorcycles* make up the compound direct object.]

NOTE The direct object may come before the verb.

DO   V

EXAMPLE What a beautiful **song** she played! [Played what? Played a song. *Song* is the direct object.]

EXERCISE B Underline the direct object in each of the sentences below. Remember to underline all parts of a compound direct object.

Examples 1. The small, fragrant flowers attracted <u>bumblebees</u> and other <u>insects</u>. [Attracted what? Attracted bumblebees and insects. *Bumblebees* and *insects* make up the compound direct object.]

     2. The bakery sells fresh <u>bread</u> and <u>muffins</u>. [Sells what? Sells bread and muffins. *Bread* and *muffins* make up the compound direct object.]

11. Bring glue or tape for the project. [Which words answer the question *Bring what?*]

12. What a great smile you have! [Which word answers the question *Have what?*]

13. Simon called Clara Ruiz and Kate Samson last night.

14. During the course of a year, the class will read several novels, short stories, plays, essays, and poems.

15. The geometry problems fascinated me.

16. After dinner, we cleaned the pots and pans.

17. The speech inspired the crowd.

18. Did anyone lose a scarf or a jacket?

19. Please, empty the recycling bin and the trash can.

20. Our cat sharpens its claws on the fence post.

Third Course

Indirect Objects

2k. An ***indirect object*** is a noun, pronoun, or word group that often appears in sentences containing direct objects. An indirect object tells *to whom* or *to what* (or *for whom* or *for what*) the action of a transitive verb is done.

                                       V IO   DO

EXAMPLES   Toss **him** the football. [Toss the football to whom? To him. *Him* is the indirect object.]

                                       V   IO   DO

The rancher brought the **cattle** some hay. [Brought hay to what? To the cattle. *Cattle* is the indirect object.]

                                       V   IO   DO

Uncle Max built my **parents** an entertainment center. [Built an entertainment center for whom? For parents. *Parents* is the indirect object.]

NOTE Don't mistake an *object of a preposition* for an indirect object. A noun or pronoun that follows *to* or *for* is part of a prepositional phrase and is not an indirect object.

                                       V   DO   OP

EXAMPLES   Patrick tossed the football **to Willis.** [*Willis* is the object of the preposition *to.*]

                                       V   DO   OP

The rancher brought some hay **to** the **cattle.** [*Cattle* is the object of the preposition *to.*]

                                       V   DO   OP

Uncle Max built an entertainment center **for** my **parents.** [*Parents* is the object of the preposition *for.*]

EXERCISE A Underline the indirect object in each of the following sentences. Remember that the indirect object will not be part of a prepositional phrase.

Examples 1. Did you save Aaron a baked potato? [Did you save a baked potato for whom? For Aaron. *Aaron* is the indirect object.]

        2. Ms. Morrow taught them the lesson about the stock market. [Ms. Morrow taught the lesson to whom? To them. *Them* is the indirect object.]

1. I brought Debbie a surprise. [Which word answers the question *I brought a surprise to whom?*]

2. The waitress served everyone at the table a plate of food. [Which word answers the question *The waitress served a plate to whom?*]

3. The noise from the construction site gave me a headache.

4. Will you lend Karen your pencil?

5. On Saturday, the teenagers built the children a wooden fort.

6. Why did your dog bring me this pair of socks?

7. For Sue's birthday, Aunt Jean gave her a book of poems.

8. Will you buy Maurice a sandwich at the lunch counter?

9. Did Ramona lend you her book?

10. Phillip, hand Sasha that paintbrush beside your sketch pad.

Compound Indirect Objects

An action verb may have more than one indirect object. Two or more indirect objects that tell *to whom* or *to what* (or *for whom* or *for what*) the action of the transitive verb is done are called a *compound indirect object.*

                            V   **IO**   **IO**   **DO**

EXAMPLE The rancher brought the **cows** and **horses** some hay. [Brought hay to what? To the cows and horses. The compound indirect object is *cows* and *horses*.]

EXERCISE B Underline the compound indirect object in each of the following sentences.

Examples 1. Give the actors and director the award. [Give the award to whom? To the *actors* and *director.*]

        2. My little cousin blew my sister and me a kiss. [Blew a kiss to whom? To my *sister* and *me.*]

11. Tara bought Spotty and Skeeter new chew toys. [Which words answer the question *Tara bought chew toys for whom?*]

12. Did the lawn mower give you and your sister problems? [Which words answer the question *The lawn mower did give problems to whom?*]

13. The dressmaker sewed Marla and Nancy new dresses.

14. Their involvement in the community earned Isabel and Alex nominations for Volunteer of the Year.

15. Mail each student and teacher an invitation.

16. Kimi showed Lee and Fred pictures from her vacation.

17. Greg's parrot gave Jill and me a strange look.

18. Send Carrie and Leo a copy of the directions.

19. Uncle Luke made my brother and me dinner.

20. The carpenter built the teacher and principal bookshelves.

Classifying Sentences by Purpose

2l. A sentence may be classified, depending on its purpose, as *declarative, imperative, interrogative,* or *exclamatory.*

(1) A *declarative sentence* makes a statement and ends with a period.

> **EXAMPLES** I saw a hot-air balloon today. [statement]
>
> The poet John Keats lived only twenty-five years. [statement]

(2) An *imperative sentence* gives a command or makes a request. Most imperative sentences end with a period. A strong command ends with an exclamation point.

> **EXAMPLES** Look at those hot-air balloons. [command]
>
> Please read one of Keats's poems aloud. [request]
>
> Help me! [strong command]

TIP Often, when people state a strong command, they speak more loudly than when they state a simple command or make a request. When you write, you can show this change in volume by using an exclamation point.

> **EXAMPLES** Please be quiet. [request]   Be quiet! [strong command]

NOTE The subject of a command is always *you.* When *you* doesn't appear in imperative sentences, *you* is called the *understood subject.*

> **EXAMPLES** (You) Look at those hot-air balloons. [command]
>
> (You) Please read one of Keats's poems aloud. [request]
>
> (You) Help me! [strong command]

The word *you* is the understood subject even when the person spoken to is addressed by name.

> **EXAMPLE** Lucinda, (you) please bring me a fork. [In this request, *Lucinda* is used to get the listener's attention. *You,* not *Lucinda,* is the subject.]

EXERCISE A On the line provided, write *DEC* if the sentence is *declarative* or *IMP* if the sentence is *imperative.*

Examples __DEC__ **1.** Poets write about love, sadness, and even laziness. [statement]

__IMP__ **2.** Listen to this! [strong command]

_____ **1.** I will get the anthology of poetry from the top shelf. [Is this sentence a statement or a command?]

_____ **2.** Watch out for that falling book! [Is this sentence a statement or a command?]

_____ **3.** Open your book to the section on Romantic poets.

_____ **4.** The term "Romantic" does not refer only to love.

_____ **5.** Romantic poetry values the feelings and emotions of the poet.

_____ **6.** Imagine a field of golden daffodils.

GO ON ➡

_____ **7.** An important quality of Romantic poetry is imagination.

_____ **8.** Please tell me the names of at least two Romantic poets.

_____ **9.** Hurry!

_____**10.** In the late 1700s and early 1800s, Romantic poetry flourished.

---

(3) An *interrogative sentence* asks a question and ends with a question mark.

> **EXAMPLES** Do you know Spanish**?** [This sentence asks a question.]
>
> How did you learn a foreign language**?** [This sentence asks a question.]

(4) An *exclamatory sentence* shows excitement or expresses strong feeling and ends with an exclamation point.

> **EXAMPLES** I won the contest**!** [This sentence shows excitement.]
>
> What a lovely dress that is**!** [This sentence expresses strong feeling.]

EXERCISE B Punctuate each sentence below with an appropriate end mark: a period, a question mark, or an exclamation point. Then, on the line provided, classify each sentence by writing *DEC* for *declarative, IMP* for *imperative, INT* for *interrogative,* or *EXC* for *exclamatory.*

Examples __INT__ **1.** What are you talking about**?** [This sentence asks a question.]

__EXC__ **2.** What a fabulous time we had**!** [This sentence expresses strong feeling.]

_____**11.** Where are the posters for our campaign [Does this sentence express strong feeling or ask a question?]

_____**12.** Don't touch that sharp edge [Is this sentence a statement or a command?]

_____**13.** I can't believe I did so well on that test

_____**14.** For several weeks, I have been knitting a sweater

_____**15.** Come with us to the movie theater

_____**16.** How often do you practice your golf swing

_____**17.** What a marvelous idea you have

_____**18.** This summer, Emily became one of my best friends

_____**19.** Will you make whole-wheat waffles for breakfast tomorrow

_____**20.** Look out

The Prepositional Phrase A

A *phrase* is a group of related words that is used as a single part of speech. A phrase does not contain both a subject and a verb.

The Prepositional Phrase

3b. A *prepositional phrase* includes a preposition, the object of the preposition, and any modifiers of that object.

> **EXAMPLES** in the book   under a wide umbrella   through a dark tunnel

3c. The noun or pronoun in a prepositional phrase is called the *object of the preposition.*

>   **OP**
> **EXAMPLES** **In the closet,** I found the broom. [*Closet* is the object of the preposition *in.*]
>
>   **OP**   **OP**
> I swept **under Roger's desk and a chair.** [*Desk* and *chair* form the compound object of the preposition *under.*]

EXERCISE A Underline each prepositional phrase in the following sentences. Remember to include all parts of a compound object. Then, draw a second line under each object of a preposition. Some sentences contain more than one prepositional phrase.

Example 1. The canvas sails snapped in the wind from the sea. [*Wind* is the object of the

preposition *in. Sea* is the object of the preposition *from.*]

1. Can you read the name on the blue boat? [What is the object of the preposition *on*?]

2. Early in the morning, Earl fishes for shrimp.

3. Often, he also looks for crabs and lobsters.

4. The storm at sea probably will not come near our coastal town.

5. Look at the beautiful sailboat in the harbor!

The Adjective Phrase

3d. A prepositional phrase that modifies a noun or a pronoun is called an *adjective phrase.*

An adjective phrase answers the same questions that an adjective answers: *What kind? Which one? How many?* or *How much?* Adjective phrases usually follow the nouns or pronouns they modify, and more than one adjective phrase may modify the same word.

> **EXAMPLES** We're reading a play **by Shakespeare about Julius Caesar.** [The prepositional phrases *by Shakespeare* and *about Julius Caesar* each indicate which play.]
>
> Is Brutus the hero **of the play**? [The prepositional phrase *of the play* identifies which hero.]

EXERCISE B Underline each adjective phrase in the following sentences. Then, draw an arrow from the adjective phrase to the noun or pronoun the phrase modifies. Some sentences contain more than one adjective phrase.

Examples 1. Does the light fixture inside the storage closet need a new bulb? [*Inside the storage closet* is an adjective phrase identifying which fixture.]

2. The basketball with the lump on one side bounces wildly. [*With the lump* is an adjective phrase identifying which basketball, and *on one side* is an adjective phrase describing *lump*.]

6. Students throughout the school are happy it snowed today. [Which phrase begins with a preposition? Which noun does the phrase describe?]

7. Did your lab partner take notes about the experiment's results? [Which phrase begins with a preposition? Which noun does the phrase describe?]

8. Someone left the door to the garage open.

9. Is that my notebook near the lunch tray on the table?

10. The poster near the water fountain outside our classroom looks ancient.

11. Some people from our neighborhood are painting the sign next to the entrance.

12. Let's take the gravel path around the observatory.

13. Stories about the cost of a new bicycle frame are all too true!

14. The kingfishers along the river always chatter when they fly.

15. The fans in the stands grew quiet once they heard the national anthem.

The Prepositional Phrase B

The Adverb Phrase

3e. A prepositional phrase that modifies a verb, an adjective, or an adverb is called an *adverb phrase.*

REMINDER A prepositional phrase includes a preposition, the object of the preposition, and any modifiers of that object.

EXAMPLES   within a few seconds   above Ruby's desk   to the restaurant

An adverb phrase tells *how, when, where, why,* or *to what extent.* An adverb phrase may appear anywhere in the sentence—at its beginning, its middle, or its end.

EXAMPLES   **In an early scene,** a soothsayer warns Caesar. [The adverb phrase *In an early scene* begins the sentence and tells when a soothsayer warns Caesar.]

A soothsayer, **in an early scene,** warns Caesar. [The adverb phrase appears in the middle of the sentence.]

A soothsayer warns Caesar **in an early scene.** [The adverb phrase appears at the end of the sentence.]

EXERCISE A Underline each adverb phrase in the following sentences. Some sentences contain more than one adverb phrase. Be careful not to underline any adjective phrases.

Examples 1. Since sunset, only one lone coyote has howled. [*Since sunset* is an adverb phrase telling when the coyote howled.]

2. On her vacation, Chi sent me this postcard of Padre Island. [*On her vacation* is an adverb phrase telling when the postcard was sent. *Of Padre Island* is not an adverb phrase; it is an adjective phrase modifying the noun *postcard.*]

1. Because of rust, the gate in the stone wall would not open. [Which of the two prepositional phrases is an adverb phrase explaining why?]

2. Darcy has always been great at shortstop. [Which phrase is an adverb phrase explaining how?]

3. During the morning, the horses walked in Central Park.

4. Before the game, do the cheerleaders practice their cheers?

5. You can stay for a few days in our apartment.

6. Allergies have left Paulette's voice hoarse beyond description.

7. We followed the fossil dinosaur tracks into the streambed.

8. The loudest of the seven frogs lives among those reeds.

9. This clip, according to the manual, should connect the spring to the hood.

10. Just drag the nylon line across the creek's surface.

GO ON

EXERCISE B Underline each adverb phrase in the following sentences. Then, draw an arrow from the adverb phrase to the verb, adjective, or adverb that the phrase modifies. Some sentences have more than one adverb phrase. Be careful not to underline any adjective phrases modifying nouns or pronouns.

Examples 1. Before his race, Joseph rose to his feet and stretched his calves. [*Before his race* describes when Joseph rose and stretched, and *to his feet* describes how he rose.]

2. The load in the trailer has shifted toward the cab. [*Toward the cab* describes where the load has shifted. *In the trailer* modifies the noun *load*, so it is an adjective phrase.]

11. Yolanda is wonderful in the play's leading role. [What adjective describing Yolanda does the prepositional phrase modify?]

12. We left for the museum at nine o'clock. [Which prepositional phrase tells where and modifies the verb? Which prepositional phrase tells when and modifies the verb?]

13. Were the costumes finished in time for the fair?

14. On spring afternoons, thunderstorms form throughout this region.

15. This glass is slick across its surface.

16. Skilled with computers, Daisy wrote a program that generates model atoms.

17. This net should be large enough for several hundred prom-night balloons.

18. On our trip, we journeyed past a huge statue of Paul Bunyan.

19. This fireplace, before the first big cold snap, seemed uncalled-for.

20. Melanie felt enthusiastic about her sister's medical research.

The Participle and the Participial Phrase
The Participle

3f. A *participle* is a verb form that can be used as an adjective.

> **EXAMPLES** a **winning** attitude [The participle *winning* describes the noun *attitude*.]
>
> the **folded** page [The participle *folded* describes the noun *page*.]
>
> the **chosen** few [The participle *chosen* describes the pronoun *few*.]

NOTE There are two kinds of participles: *present participles* and *past participles*. All present participles end in *–ing*. Past participles may end in *–ed* or *–en* or *–t;* however, some past participles are formed in other ways.

> **EXAMPLES** Zippy chased the **rolling** ball. [*Rolling* is a present participle describing *ball*.]
>
> The doghouse, **painted** blue, sat under a tree. [The past participle *painted* describes *doghouse*.]
>
> Will this **blown** gasket need to be replaced? [*Blown* describes *gasket*.]

REMINDER Although participles can be used as adjectives, they often appear in verb phrases. When a participle is joined to a helping verb in a verb phrase, it is part of the verb and is not an adjective.

> **EXAMPLE** Zippy **had been playing** with a ball. [*Playing* is a present participle. *Had* and *been* are helping verbs. Together they form the verb phrase *had been playing*. In this sentence, *playing* is not used as an adjective.]

EXERCISE A Underline any participles that are used as adjectives in the following sentences. Then, draw an arrow from the participle to the noun or pronoun the participle modifies.

Example 1. The ball slipped past the first puzzled batter. [*Puzzled* is a past participle describing *batter*.]

1. Ada's exhausted teammates sat together on the bench. [Which word is a past participle? Which plural noun does it describe?]

2. Her hushed friends watched Ada step to the plate.

3. Suddenly, a speeding runner stole third base.

4. The pitcher threw a wavering curveball right down the middle.

5. Ada hit it solidly and drove in the winning run.

GO ON

The Participial Phrase

3g. A *participial phrase* is used as an adjective and consists of a participle and any complements or modifiers the participle has.

> **EXAMPLES** Harry put the invitations, **written on red paper,** in his friends' lockers. [The participial phrase consists of the participle *written* and the adverb phrase *on red paper.*]
>
> Four **recently built** aircraft are ready for test flights. [The participial phrase consists of the participle *built* and the adverb *recently.*]

EXERCISE B Underline the participial phrases in the following sentences. Then, draw an arrow from each participial phrase to the noun or pronoun the phrase modifies. A sentence may have more than one participial phrase.

Examples 1. Covered in pink blossoms, the peach tree was beautiful. [The participial phrase *Covered in pink blossoms* modifies *tree.*]

2. Does this curiously shaped hedge need to be trimmed? [The participial phrase *curiously shaped* modifies *hedge.*]

6. The bus stopped next to a building surrounded by statues. [Which words are parts of the participial phrase? What noun does the participial phrase modify?]

7. Re-reading my essay, I discovered that two words were missing. [Which words are parts of the participial phrase? What pronoun does the participial phrase modify?]

8. The light cast by the aquarium's fluorescent bulb was bright.

9. During the recital, several parents chuckled at their wildly dancing toddlers.

10. Baked with cinnamon, the apples were delicious.

11. How many birds living in this open field have you identified?

12. Opening the blinds, Ms. Saadi faced the newly risen sun.

13. The cowboy's story, sprinkled with wit, kept his audience happy.

14. Snuffling noisily together, the hounds explored an old shoe.

15. How long do closely guarded secrets really stay secret?

The Gerund and the Gerund Phrase
The Gerund

3h.   A *gerund* is a verb form ending in *–ing* that is used as a noun.

EXAMPLES   **Roaring** filled the air at the track. [*Roaring* is a gerund used as the subject.]

Most of it was **cheering.** [*Cheering* is a gerund used as the predicate nominative.]

We could hear **thundering.** [*Thundering* is a gerund used as a direct object.]

Still, fans gave **applauding** their full attention. [*Applauding* is a gerund used as an indirect object.]

When the cars entered the track, we turned our attention toward **racing.** [*Racing* is a gerund used as the object of a preposition.]

NOTE▶ The present participle forms end in *–ing* and can function as gerunds, participles, or verbs. If the *–ing* word is used as a noun, it is a gerund. If the *–ing* word is used as an adjective, it is a participle. If the *–ing* word is part of a verb phrase, it is a verb.

EXAMPLES   **Humming,** Aunt Tammy enjoyed **cooking.** [*Humming* is used as an adjective describing *Aunt Tammy*, so it is a present participle. *Cooking* tells what Aunt Tammy enjoyed and is used as a noun, so it must be a gerund.]

Sweating, Latisha and her brother **were painting** her home for **showing.** [*Sweating* is used as an adjective describing *Latisha* and her *brother*, so it is a present participle. *Painting* is part of the verb phrase *were painting*, so it is a verb. *Showing* is the object of the preposition *for*, so it is a gerund.]

EXERCISE A Underline the gerunds in the following sentences.

Example   1. After he gets a story idea, Manuel likes writing. [*Writing* is a gerund used as the sentence's direct object.]

1. Whitney's favorite part of basketball is dunking. [Which word ends in *–ing* and is a gerund used as a predicate nominative?]

2. Because three kittens live here, our home is often filled with mewing and meowing.

3. Catching is one of the first skills we teach young ballplayers.

4. Bruce, give practicing a little more of your time.

5. Their singing impressed Lucinda.

GO ON ▶

The Gerund Phrase

3i.   A *gerund phrase* consists of a gerund and any modifiers or complements the gerund has. The entire phrase is used as a noun.

> **EXAMPLES**   **The loud beeping in the kitchen** was the smoke alarm. [*The, loud,* and *in the kitchen* are modifiers of the gerund *beeping*. The entire phrase is used as the subject of the sentence.]
>
> This cat enjoys **carrying scraps of paper to us.** [The gerund *carrying* is followed by its complement, *scraps*, and the modifiers, *of paper* and *to us*. The entire gerund phrase is used as the direct object of the verb *enjoys*.]

EXERCISE B Underline the gerund phrase in each of the following sentences. Then, draw a second line under the gerund.

Examples 1. Creatively doodling in her notebook helps Lori relax. [The gerund phrase *Creatively doodling in her notebook* functions as the subject of the sentence. The adverb *Creatively* and the adverb phrase *in her notebook* modify the gerund *doodling*.]

2. I always look forward to Aunt Tammy's delicious cooking. [The gerund phrase *Aunt Tammy's delicious cooking* functions as the object of the preposition *to. Aunt Tammy's* and *delicious* modify the gerund *cooking*.]

6. The choir gave preparing for the concert their full attention. [Which words help to modify the gerund *preparing*?]

7. Slowly and carefully detailing his car is Kim's favorite task. [Which words help to modify the gerund *detailing*? Which words help to complete the gerund's meaning?]

8. Would you help me with hanging these posters?

9. The ball's bouncing into the stands surprised everyone.

10. The firefighter's heroic act was daringly rescuing an entire family.

11. Clara's latest amusement is cheaply collecting memorabilia from the seventies.

12. We practiced quickly passing the ball to our forwards.

13. Boiling gently in water will cook the pasta.

14. Who hasn't enjoyed heartily laughing at one comedian or another?

15. A distant clattering along the rails was the first sign of the subway car's approach.

The Infinitive and the Infinitive Phrase
The Infinitive

3j. An *infinitive* is a verb form that can be used as a noun, an adjective, or an adverb. Most infinitives begin with *to.*

NOUN   **To sing** was her only desire. [*To sing* is the subject of the verb *was.*]

Our three history instructors really like **to teach.** [*To teach* is the direct object of the verb *like.* Instructors like what? Like to teach.]

His greatest hope is **to win.** [*To win* renames the subject, *hope.*]

ADJECTIVE   The song **to sing** is "Unchained Melody." [*To sing* tells which song.]

ADVERB   She was inspired **to sing** by Whitney Houston. [*To sing* tells how she was inspired.]

EXERCISE A Underline the infinitive in each of the following sentences. Then, if the infinitive is used as an adjective or an adverb, draw an arrow from the infinitive to the word it modifies.

Example 1. Sweet to taste, the honey was fresh from the honeycomb. [*To taste* is an adverb modifying the adjective *Sweet.*]

1. One book to read is *Cranford* by Elizabeth Gaskell. [Is the infinitive used as a noun or does it modify a noun?]

2. After I'd laced up my high-tops, I was eager to play.

3. Is a foreign language easy to learn?

4. Ready to run, members of the track team lined up at their marks.

5. To cook is not a simple task.

The Infinitive Phrase

3k. An *infinitive phrase* consists of an infinitive and any modifiers or complements the infinitive has. The entire phrase can be used as a noun, an adjective, or an adverb.

NOUN   Tara learned **to sculpt in clay.** [The infinitive phrase is used as a direct object. Tara learned what? Learned to sculpt in clay. The adverb phrase *in clay* modifies the infinitive *to sculpt.*]

ADJECTIVE   Tara's desire **to sculpt marine animals** began after she visited an aquarium. [The infinitive phrase modifies the noun *desire* and tells which desire. The infinitive *to sculpt* has a direct object, *marine animals.*]

ADVERB   Tara displays her sculptures **to sell them.** [The infinitive phrase modifies the verb *displays* and tells why she displays her sculptures.]

NOTE The word *to* begins both infinitive and prepositional phrases. Generally, when a verb form follows *to*, the word group is an infinitive, and when a noun or pronoun follows *to*, the word group is a prepositional phrase.

INFINITIVE PHRASE The lioness ran **to reach her cubs.** [*To* is followed by the verb form *reach*. *To reach* is an infinitive used as an adverb explaining why the lioness ran.]

PREPOSITIONAL PHRASE The lioness ran **to her cubs.** [*To* is followed by the object of the prepositional phrase, *cubs,* and the modifier of *cubs, her. To her cubs* is an adverb phrase explaining where the lioness ran.]

EXERCISE B Underline the infinitive or infinitive phrase in each of the following sentences. Then, if the infinitive or infinitive phrase is used as an adjective or an adverb, draw two lines under the word or words it modifies.

Examples 1. After working a long shift, Ryan wanted to sleep. [*To sleep* is used as a noun; it is the direct object. Ryan wanted what? He wanted to sleep.]

      2. Are you making those posters to help Isabel? [*To help Isabel* is used as an adverb explaining why you are making posters.]

6. To make his wheelchair go forward, Chris presses on this lever. [Does the infinitive phrase act as a noun, or does it modify a verb?]

7. At the playoffs, her dream to photograph sports stars was fulfilled. [Does the infinitive phrase act as a noun, or does it modify a noun?]

8. Your next responsibility is to make good grades in school.

9. To entertain was the juggler's goal for each performance.

10. The pill bug has the ability to roll itself into a tiny ball.

11. Stock these shelves carefully to keep the soup cans from falling.

12. Was this software designed to create new Web pages?

13. David and Alma want to try out for roles in *Our Town.*

14. Either red pepper or curry powder is a suitable spice to use in that recipe.

15. We need to carry these boxes of files to the office.

The Appositive and the Appositive Phrase
The Appositive

3l. An *appositive* is a noun or a pronoun placed beside another noun or pronoun to identify or describe it.

> **EXAMPLES** When is Ms. Fisk, the **principal,** visiting our class? [The appositive *principal* follows and identifies the proper noun *Ms. Fisk.*]
>
> A **lute,** this ancient pear-shaped instrument has eleven strings. [The appositive *lute* precedes and describes the noun *instrument.*]

EXERCISE A Underline the appositive in each of the following sentences. Then, draw an arrow from the appositive to the noun or pronoun it identifies or describes.

Examples 1. Jeremy, a golfer, entered the competition. [*Golfer* describes *Jeremy.*]

2. The space shuttle *Columbia* carried *Spacelab* into space. [*Columbia* identifies *shuttle.*]

1. My home state, Oregon, is on the West Coast. [Which word identifies *state*?]

2. The country Japan is a group of islands in the Pacific Ocean. [Which word identifies *country*?]

3. Have you ever seen photographs of her, Justice Sandra Day O'Connor?

4. Deliver this gift, a houseplant, to our new neighbors.

5. The athlete Carl Lewis won nine Olympic gold medals in track and field.

6. Glimpses of his own past helped transform the penny-pincher Scrooge into a new person.

7. Connect this belt to the part of the alternator that fits it, the pulley.

8. Gottlieb Daimler and Wilhelm Maybach, German engineers, built a motorized bicycle in 1885.

9. Safely landing the lunar module *Eagle*, Neil Armstrong and Edwin E. Aldrin, Jr., became the first people to walk on the moon.

10. During the Roaring Twenties, the Jazz Age, many Americans ignored distress in Europe.

The Appositive Phrase

3m. An *appositive phrase* consists of an appositive and any modifiers it has.

> **EXAMPLES** Ms. Davis, **the principal of this large high school,** will see you now. [The article *the* and the prepositional phrase *of this large high school* modify the appositive *principal.* The entire phrase follows and identifies *Ms. Davis.*]

GO ON

> **Principal of our high school,** Ms. Davis sets rules and procedures. [The prepositional phrase *of our high school* modifies the appositive *Principal.* The entire phrase precedes and identifies *Ms. Davis.*]

NOTE Commas set off an appositive or appositive phrase that is not necessary to the meaning of the sentence. Commas generally do not set off an appositive that is necessary to the meaning of the sentence or is part of someone's name.

> **EXAMPLES** Vincent Van Gogh, **the painter of *Olive Trees*,** once worked as a preacher in Belgium. [The appositive phrase is not necessary to the meaning of the sentence, so it is set off with commas.]
>
> The painter **Vincent van Gogh** once worked as a preacher in Belgium. [Without the appositive, we would not know which painter once worked as a preacher in Belgium. The appositive is necessary to the meaning of the sentence, so it is not set off with commas.]

EXERCISE B Underline the appositive or appositive phrase in each of the following sentences. Then, draw an arrow from the appositive or appositive phrase to the noun or pronoun to which it refers.

Examples 1. My friend Tammy Benson is known for her funny poems. [*Tammy Benson* identifies *friend.*]

2. Does Miller Road, the long route to your house, curve around a duck pond? [*The long route to your house* describes *Miller Road.*]

11. Volcanoes, the subject of my report, are vents in the earth's crust. [Which word group refers to *Volcanoes*?]

12. Use one of those, the lockers in the bottom row, for your gym clothes. [Which word group identifies *those*?]

13. Did all of them enjoy the main dish, a mix of vegetables and pasta?

14. Find the brightest planet, the hot-surfaced Venus, in the night sky.

15. A small, five-armed creature with a spiny skeleton, a starfish, washed ashore.

16. The busy highway the Lincoln Turnpike is undergoing repairs this week.

17. Robert Browning wrote *The Ring and the Book*, the tale of a Roman trial.

18. My friends and I like salsa, a fast and energetic kind of dance music.

19. Did you hear that, a loud buzzing outside the window?

20. Captain of the team, Mel decided the batters' lineup.

The Adjective Clause

4d. An *adjective clause* is a subordinate clause that modifies a noun or pronoun.

REMINDER▶ A *subordinate clause* is a word group that has a subject and a verb but cannot stand alone as a sentence.

SUBORDINATE CLAUSES   as we waited for sunrise [The clause contains the subject *we* and the verb *waited*, but it does not express a complete thought.]

after the sun set [The clause contains the subject *sun* and the verb *set*, but it does not express a complete thought.]

SENTENCES   As we waited for sunrise, we watched a meteor shower. [The subordinate clause adds information to an independent clause.]

We watched a meteor shower after the sun set. [The subordinate clause adds information to an independent clause.]

Like an adjective, an adjective clause modifies a noun or pronoun by telling *what kind* or *which one*. An adjective clause usually follows the noun or pronoun it modifies.

EXAMPLES   I want a necklace **that has a blue stone.** [*That has a blue stone* modifies *necklace* by telling what kind.]

Her ring, **which was a gift,** has a green stone. [*Which was a gift* modifies *ring* by telling which one.]

EXERCISE A A noun or pronoun in each of the following sentences is underlined. Draw two lines under the adjective clause that describes the underlined noun or pronoun.

Example 1. Take the <u>watch</u> that Grandpa gave you to the repair shop. [*That Grandpa gave you* tells which watch.]

1. The <u>people</u> who read that book didn't like the story's ending. [Which word group tells what kind of people?]

2. I spoke to <u>Aaron</u>, whose locker is near mine, after study hall.

3. Have you seen the action <u>movie</u> that opened on Friday?

4. The <u>spot</u> where we build the campfire should be in an open area.

5. Meet <u>Anya</u>, whom you will tutor for English class.

Relative Pronouns

An adjective clause usually begins with a relative pronoun. The relative pronoun relates the adjective clause to the word or words the clause describes. Common relative pronouns are *who, whom, whose, which,* and *that.*

EXAMPLES   A scientist **whom I admire** is George Washington Carver. [*Whom* relates the clause to *scientist.*]

GO ON ▶

Carver developed new products **that were made from peanuts.** [*That* relates the clause to *products.*]

The words *where* and *when* may also introduce an adjective clause. When used to introduce an adjective clause, these words are called *relative adverbs.* Like relative pronouns, relative adverbs relate the clause to the word or words the clause modifies.

EXAMPLE The school **where Carver taught** is now named Tuskegee University. [*Where* relates the clause to *school.*]

EXERCISE B Underline the adjective clause in each of the following sentences. Then, draw an arrow from the adjective clause to the word the clause modifies.

Examples 1. Carver directed an experimental farm where crops were tested. [*Where* relates the adjective clause to *farm.*]

2. One crop that Carver studied during the late 1800s was soybeans. [*That* relates the adjective clause to *crop.*]

6. Carver was born in a time when slavery was still practiced. [Which clause begins with a relative adverb? Which word does the clause describe?]

7. Is the war that ended legal slavery in the United States the Civil War? [Which clause begins with a relative pronoun? Which word does the clause describe?]

8. In his late twenties, Carver, who had held a variety of odd jobs, graduated from high school.

9. His artistic skills surfaced during his childhood, which he spent on a plantation.

10. As a boy Carver learned to draw, and as he grew older, he painted pictures of the plants that grew around him.

11. Carver, whose college degree was in agricultural science, first studied art and piano.

12. Is Carver a scholar whom you would imitate?

13. The place where he earned his bachelor's degree was Iowa State Agricultural College.

14. Tell me about the master of science degree that he earned in 1896.

15. He donated his life savings to the Carver Research Foundation, which he helped establish.

The Adverb Clause

4e. An *adverb clause* is a subordinate clause that modifies a verb, an adjective, or an adverb.

REMINDER A *subordinate clause* is a word group that has a subject and a verb but cannot stand alone as a sentence.

An adverb clause tells *how, when, where, why, how much, to what extent*, or *under what conditions*. An adverb clause can appear before or after the word or words it describes.

> **EXAMPLES** **If Todd sinks this basket,** we will win the game. [The clause modifies the verb phrase *will win* by telling under what condition we will win.]
>
> Did he call me **while I was out**? [The clause modifies the verb phrase *Did call* by asking when he did call.]
>
> This canyon is deeper **than the nearby canyons are.** [The clause modifies the adjective *deeper* by telling to what extent the canyon is deeper.]
>
> The sailor tied the knot as tightly **as he could.** [The clause modifies the adverb *tightly* by telling how tightly the sailor tied the knot.]

NOTE A comma generally sets off an adverb clause that begins a sentence. Commas do not generally set off an adverb clause that appears elsewhere in a sentence.

> **EXAMPLES** **Because I baked a casserole,** we stayed home for dinner. [The adverb clause begins the sentence, so it is set off with a comma.]
>
> We stayed home for dinner **because I baked a casserole.** [The adverb clause appears at the end of the sentence, so it is not set off with a comma.]

EXERCISE A In each of the following sentences, a verb, adjective, or adverb is underlined. Draw two lines under the adverb clause that modifies the underlined verb, adjective, or adverb.

Example 1. This year Rachel is <u>happier</u> than she was last year. [The clause describes *happier* by telling how much happier Rachel is.]

1. Kimi moves as <u>gracefully</u> as professional dancers do. [Which clause modifies *gracefully*?]

2. If you have already read this book, <u>do</u> not <u>tell</u> me the conclusion.

3. Coach has made volleyball practice sessions <u>longer</u> so that we'll get better.

4. Derek <u>plays</u> songs on the guitar whenever he is feeling cheerful.

5. Since you know French, <u>will</u> you <u>translate</u> this for me?

GO ON

Subordinating Conjunctions

Adverb clauses are introduced by *subordinating conjunctions*. A subordinating conjunction shows the relationship between the adverb clause and the word or words the clause describes.

COMMON SUBORDINATING CONJUNCTIONS

after	as long as	even though	since	unless	where
although	as soon as	if	so that	until	wherever
as	because	in order that	than	when	whether
as if	before	once	though	whenever	while

> **EXAMPLES** We will plant this tree **where the sun shines most brightly.** [The subordinating conjunction *where* introduces an adverb clause modifying the verb *will plant*. The clause tells where we will plant the tree.]
>
> Is Kayla taller **than Al is?** [The subordinating conjunction *than* introduces an adverb clause modifying the adjective *taller*. The clause asks if Kayla is taller.]

NOTE▶ Some subordinating conjunctions, such as *after, before, since,* and *until,* may also be used as prepositions. Remember that an adverb clause will contain both a subject and a verb.

> **EXAMPLES** Feed the dog **before you go to school.** [The clause has a both a subject, *you,* and a verb, *go,* so it is an adverb clause.]
> Feed the dog **before school.** [The prepositional phrase has no subject or verb, so it is not an adverb clause.]

EXERCISE B Underline the adverb clause in each of the following sentences.

Example 1. This old bridge got rustier <u>while we were away</u>. [The clause modifies *got* by telling when the bridge got rustier.]

6. Before Sue took her palomino to the horse show, she groomed the horse carefully. [Which clause modifies the verb *groomed*?]

7. Was the golden retriever friendlier than the Great Dane was?

8. If the weather is cold, we will exercise inside the gym.

9. The brothers usually behave as if they are best friends.

10. Shannon painted slowly so that the brush strokes were distinct.

Third Course

The Noun Clause

4f.	A *noun clause* is a subordinate clause that is used as a noun.

REMINDER ▶ A *subordinate clause* is a word group that has a subject and a verb but cannot stand alone as a sentence.

Like a noun, a noun clause can be used as a subject or as a predicate nominative.

SUBJECT   **Why the ship sank** is a mystery. [The clause tells what the sentence is about.]

PREDICATE NOMINATIVE   The mystery is **why the ship sank.** [The clause follows a linking verb and renames the subject, *mystery.*]

Noun clauses are usually introduced by one of the following words:

that	whatever	whenever	whether	whoever	whomever
what	when	where	who	whom	why

EXAMPLES   The basketball court is **where you'll find Zack.** [The clause is introduced by *where* and identifies the subject, *court.*]

Who serves as class president will be up to the voters. [The clause is introduced by *Who* and functions as the subject.]

EXERCISE A Underline the noun clause in each of the following sentences.

Examples   **1.** Is daily practice <u>why she plays tennis so well</u>? [The clause is introduced by *why* and identifies the subject, *practice.*]

     2. <u>When the sun has just set</u> is the best time to catch fireflies. [The clause is introduced by *when* and functions as the subject of this sentence.]

1. Does what the parrot says make you laugh? [Which clause is introduced by *what* and functions as the subject?]

2. The scientist's only concern was whether the experiment was a success. [Which clause is introduced by *whether* and renames the subject, *concern*?]

3. That the plan worked surprised us both.

4. The trouble with the engine is what I expected.

5. Whoever chooses to report on this book will get an extra week to finish reading it.

6. According to Beth, quick and accurate revision is why she uses that program.

7. Whatever venture Rosa supports becomes successful.

8. Is whoever moved the queen's crown still in the palace?

9. The show's finest moments were when the magician pretended to read minds.

10. "Where the trail ends" is our club's new slogan.

Like a noun, a noun clause can also be used as a direct object, an indirect object, or as the object of a preposition.

DIRECT OBJECT	Tell me **why the ship sank.** [The clause answers the question *Tell me what?*]
INDIRECT OBJECT	I will give **why the ship sank** some thought. [The clause answers the question *Will give some thought to what?*]
OBJECT OF A PREPOSITION	Do you have an explanation for **why the ship sank**? [The clause is the object of the preposition *for. For* shows the relationship between the clause and *explanation.*]

EXERCISE B Underline the noun clause in each of the following sentences.

Examples 1. Do you know whether *Hatchet* by Gary Paulsen is a true story? [The clause answers the question *Do know what?*]

2. I keep some money in a savings account for whenever I might need it. [The clause is the object of the preposition *for.*]

11. After an hour's hike, we found where the others had made camp. [Which clause answers the question *Found what?*]

12. Nathan gave whatever was dirty a thorough scrub. [Which clause answers the question *Gave a scrub to what?*]

13. In her writer's journal, she records whatever happens to her each day.

14. Michael gave whether he should enter the contest some serious thought.

15. According to the ranger, a bear will eat whatever it feels like eating.

16. Whoever returned her wallet deserves her thanks.

17. Set those potted plants near where the children dug the holes.

18. Ms. Ortega suddenly realized why the pack seemed heavy.

19. Do you sometimes send funny e-mails to whomever you know?

20. Give whichever hedge is too tall a trim.

Sentence Structure A

Simple Sentences

4g. Depending on its structure, a sentence can be classified as simple, compound, complex, or compound-complex.

You can identify a sentence's *structure* based on two things: (1) how many clauses are in the sentence and (2) what types of clauses they are.

REMINDER▶ A *clause* is a word group that contains a subject and its verb. An *independent clause* can stand alone as a sentence. A *subordinate clause* cannot stand alone as a sentence.

INDEPENDENT CLAUSE   Chandler sings. [The clause contains the subject *Chandler* and the verb *sings,* and it expresses a complete thought.]

SUBORDINATE CLAUSE   when he drives [The clause contains the subject *he* and the verb *drives,* but it does not express a complete thought.]

Simple sentences contain one independent clause and no subordinate clauses. They may contain compound subjects, compound verbs, and any number of phrases.

> **EXAMPLES**
>   S   V
> A **waitress brought** water to the diners. [This simple sentence has a subject, *waitress,* a verb, *brought,* and a phrase, *to the diners.* It contains one independent clause and no subordinate clauses.]
>   S   S   V   V
> The **waitress** and a **waiter brought** food and **poured** water. [This simple sentence has a compound subject, *waitress* and *waiter,* and a compound verb, *brought* and *poured.* It contains one independent clause and no subordinate clauses.]

EXERCISE A For the following sentences, draw a line under each independent clause and two lines under each subordinate clause. Then, on the line provided write *S* for *simple sentence* or *N* for *not a simple sentence.*

Example ___*S*___ **1.** Did Nicole and Clara saddle horses for a ride? [The sentence contains a compound subject, *Nicole* and *Clara,* a verb, *Did saddle,* a phrase, *for a ride,* and no subordinate clauses.]

_____ **1.** Several brushes were inside the barn. [Does the sentence have only one independent clause and no subordinate clauses?]

_____ **2.** Nicole brushed her horse Rowdy's mane, and then she cleaned his hooves, which were muddy.

_____ **3.** Is that a new saddle, or is it one of the older ones?

_____ **4.** In the pasture, a horse and her foal grazed quietly and watched Rowdy.

_____ **5.** Nearby, as Nicole brushed her horse, a barn cat and her kittens played.

GO ON ▶

Compound Sentences

Compound sentences contain two or more independent clauses and no subordinate clauses. A comma and coordinating conjunction; a semicolon; or a semicolon, a conjunctive adverb, and a comma may join independent clauses in a compound sentence.

> **EXAMPLES** Jack traveled to New York, **and** he saw the Statue of Liberty. [A comma and coordinating conjunction join the two independent clauses.]
>
> Jack enjoyed the historic city; the sights were spectacular. [A semicolon joins the two independent clauses.]
>
> He did not see a Broadway play; **however,** he will see one next summer. [A semicolon, a conjunctive adverb, and a comma join the two independent clauses.]

EXERCISE B Decide whether each sentence below is a simple sentence or a compound sentence. On the line provided, write *S* for *simple sentence* or *CD* for *compound sentence*.

Examples _____CD_____ **1.** Tato Laviera wrote "hate"; the poem comments on the dangers of hatred. [The sentence consists of two independent clauses joined with a semicolon.]

_____S_____ **2.** The writer compares hatred to a snake and warns about the poison of its first bite. [The sentence consists of one independent clause with a compound verb, *compares* and *warns.*]

_____ **6.** In my opinion, everyone gets upset occasionally. [Is there one independent clause or more than one independent clause?]

_____ **7.** Some people have difficulty with stress, but others successfully handle it. [Is there one independent clause or more than one independent clause?]

_____ **8.** What upsets you or your friends?

_____ **9.** At times, stress and disappointment lead to irritation.

_____ **10.** Do coaches and athletes have advice about stress relief?

_____ **11.** Vicky and Roland exercise daily; exercise relieves their stress.

_____ **12.** Lauren writes in her journal every evening; consequently, her stress is relieved.

_____ **13.** Do you have a close friend, and do you discuss stressful events together?

_____ **14.** Almost every day, my friends and I talk about stressful things.

_____ **15.** We help one another solve problems; in this way, we are able to manage stress.

Sentence Structure B

Complex Sentences

4g.   Depending on its structure, a sentence can be classified as simple, compound, complex, or compound-complex.

You can identify a sentence's *structure* based on two things: (1) how many clauses are in the sentence and (2) what types of clauses they are.

REMINDER A *clause* is a word group that contains a subject and its verb. An *independent clause* can stand alone as a sentence. A *subordinate clause* cannot stand alone as a sentence.

INDEPENDENT CLAUSE   Misty whispered. [The clause contains the subject *Misty* and the verb *whispered,* and it expresses a complete thought.]

SUBORDINATE CLAUSE   because his boots were outside [The clause contains the subject *boots* and the verb *were,* but it does not express a complete thought.]

Complex sentences contain one independent clause and at least one subordinate clause. In the example below, the independent clause is underlined once. Each subordinate clause is underlined twice.

                                     S   V   S   V
EXAMPLE   Although Troy wanted the latest style of shoes, he chose a less expensive pair
              S   V
that also looked good. [This complex sentence contains one independent clause and two subordinate clauses.]

TIP To determine whether a clause is subordinate or whether it is independent, look at how the clause begins. Subordinate clauses often begin with words such as *because, since, when, that, which, who,* and *whose.*

EXERCISE A For the following sentences, draw a line under each independent clause and two lines under each subordinate clause. Then, on the line provided, write *CX* for *complex sentence* or *N* for *not a complex sentence.*

Example **1.** When Alan saw the leak, he groaned because he couldn't fix it. [The

independent clause is *he groaned.* The subordinate clauses are *When Alan saw*

the leak and *because he couldn't fix it.*]

_____ **1.** Since he can't fix the leak, Alan will call a plumber. [Does the sentence contain one or more subordinate clauses?]

_____ **2.** Do you have the phone number for a reliable plumber?

_____ **3.** On Thursday afternoon, he'll leave work early so that he can meet the plumber.

_____ **4.** After the leak is fixed, he'll mop up the water because guests are coming.

_____ **5.** Tina and Anthony will arrive on Thursday and will stay for the weekend.

GO ON

Compound-Complex Sentences

Compound-complex sentences contain two or more independent clauses and at least one subordinate clause.

                        S   V   S   V   S   V
EXAMPLE When we became hungry, Gary prepared carrots, and I cooked fish. [This

sentence contains two independent clauses and one subordinate clause.]

EXERCISE B For the following sentences, draw a line under each independent clause and two lines under each subordinate clause. Then, on the line provided, write *CX* for *complex sentence* or *CD-CX* for *compound-complex sentence.*

Examples _CD-CX_ **1.** Because I am an art student, I have studied different types of pens, and

I can tell you about them. [This sentence contains two independent clauses

and one subordinate clause.]

_CX_ **2.** If you give me a large feather, I can make a quill pen that you can use.

[This sentence contains one independent clause and two subordinate clauses]

_____ **6.** Until metal pens were made in the mid-nineteenth century, people wrote with brushes

or reeds, or they used quill pens. [How many independent clauses does the sentence

contain?]

_____ **7.** After metal pens and pen tips came into use, quill pens fell out of use. [How many

independent clauses does the sentence contain?]

_____ **8.** Have you heard of John Mitchell, who invented a machine-made steel pen tip in 1828?

_____ **9.** Because a person continually dipped the pen into an ink supply, these pens could be

messy; therefore, inventors looked for a better design.

_____ **10.** In 1884, L. E. Waterman produced the fountain pen, which held the ink supply within

the pen, and the design became popular.

_____ **11.** The new ballpoint pen was released before the century ended.

_____ **12.** Some people wrote with ballpoint pens in 1895, yet Lazlo Biro designed a better model

that was used worldwide by the mid-1940s.

_____ **13.** The "biro" is similar to the older fountain pen that held a reservoir of ink.

_____ **14.** The ballpoint pen holds ink in its reservoir; because a metal ball at its tip rotates, the tip

becomes coated in ink.

_____ **15.** Did you know that soft-tip pens came into use during the 1960s?

Subject-Verb Agreement A

5b. A verb should agree in number with its subject.

A subject and verb agree when they have the same number. When a word refers to one person, place, thing, or idea, it is *singular* in number. When a word refers to more than one person, place, thing, or idea, it is *plural* in number.

(1) Singular subjects take singular verbs.

> **S** **V**
> **EXAMPLE** The **dog** across the street **barks** at squirrels. [The singular verb *barks* agrees with the singular subject *dog*. The phrase *across the street* does not affect agreement, even though the phrase comes between the subject and the verb.]

(2) Plural subjects take plural verbs.

> **S** **V**
> **EXAMPLE** The **dogs** across the street **bark** at squirrels. [The plural verb *bark* agrees with the plural subject *dogs*. The phrase *across the street* does not affect agreement, even though the phrase comes between the subject and the verb.]

NOTE▶ Verb phrases also agree with their subjects. A verb phrase is made up of a main verb and one or more helping verbs. The first helping verb in the verb phrase agrees with the subject.

> **V** **S** **V**
> **EXAMPLE** **Has** your baby **brother been napping** all afternoon? [*Has been napping* is the verb phrase. The singular verb *has* agrees with the singular subject *brother*.]

EXERCISE A Circle the verb form in parentheses that agrees with the underlined subject in each of the following sentences.

Example 1. The <u>lion</u> (*spend,* (*spends*)) much of the hot afternoon asleep. [The subject *lion* is singular, so the verb must be singular, too.]

1. During our walk through the animal preserve, a fresh <u>breeze</u> (*bring, brings*) relief from the hot sun. [Is the subject singular or plural?]

2. Our <u>parents</u> always (*remind, reminds*) us to drink plenty of water on hot days.

3. The <u>polar bears</u> (*enjoy, enjoys*) their pond of cool water.

4. Big <u>cats</u> like lions and leopards (*drinks, drink*) from watering holes.

5. (*Do, Does*) an <u>elephant</u> need a lot of water?

Compound Subjects Joined by *And*

A compound subject is made up of two or more subjects that have the same verb. Subjects joined by *and* generally take a plural verb.

GO ON ▶

>   S   S   S   V
> **EXAMPLE** Fresh **basil, vinegar, and tomatoes have been added** to this dish. [The verb phrase *have been added* agrees with the plural compound subject *basil, vinegar, and tomatoes*.]

EXERCISE B Circle the verb form in parentheses that agrees with the underlined compound subject in each of the following sentences.

Example 1. Rhonda and her father *(bakes, (bake))* their favorite herb bread. [The subjects *Rhonda and her father* are joined by *and*, so the plural verb *bake* is correct.]

6. *(Have, Has)* Marcie and Michael set the table? [Which verb agrees with the compound subject?]

7. My family and friends *(looks, look)* forward to dinner together.

8. Good conversation, healthy food, and laughter *(bring, brings)* us back to the table.

9. My older brother and I often *(talk, talks)* about our day at school.

10. Breakfast, lunch, and dinner *(is, are)* pleasant occasions in our family.

Compound Subjects with *Or* or *Nor*

For compound subjects joined by *or* or *nor*, the verb should agree with the subject nearer the verb.

>   S   S   V
> **EXAMPLES** My **parents or** my **grandfather drives** me to soccer practice on Thursdays. [The singular subject *grandfather* is nearer to the verb *drives*. The singular verb *drives* agrees with the singular subject *grandfather*.]
>   S   S   V
> My **grandfather or** my **parents drive** me to soccer practice on Thursdays. [The plural subject *parents* is nearer to the verb *drive*. The plural verb *drive* agrees with the plural subject *parents*.]

EXERCISE C Circle the verb form in parentheses that agrees with the underlined compound subject in each of the following sentences.

Example 1. *(Are, (Is))* brown or white a good color for shelves? [The singular subject *brown* and the singular subject *white* both take singular verbs, so the singular verb *Is* agrees.]

11. Neither my parents nor I *(expect, expects)* the project to be easy! [Is the subject that is nearer the verb singular or plural?]

12. *(Do, Does)* nails or screws work better in this wood?

13. Either the den or the master bedroom *(are, is)* a good place for bookshelves.

14. The pantry or the kitchen *(need, needs)* more storage space.

15. Either a dropcloth or newspapers *(protect, protects)* the carpet from paint spills.

Subject-Verb Agreement B

Indefinite Pronouns

A pronoun that does not refer to a specific person, place, thing, or idea is called an ***indefinite pronoun.*** When an indefinite pronoun is used as a subject, make sure the verb agrees with the pronoun.

5d. The following indefinite pronouns are singular:

anybody	either	neither	one
anyone	everybody	nobody	somebody
anything	everyone	no one	someone
each	everything	nothing	something

Use a singular verb to agree with these pronouns when they are used as subjects.

                     S   V

EXAMPLE   **Each** of the dogs **has** its own food bowl. [The singular verb *has* agrees with the singular subject *Each*. The phrase *of the dogs* does not affect agreement, even though it comes between the subject and the verb.]

EXERCISE A Circle the verb form in parentheses that agrees with the underlined subject in each of the following sentences.

Example 1. <u>Everyone</u> (*tries*, *try*) his or her hardest on the test. [The indefinite pronoun *Everyone* is singular, so the verb should be singular, too.]

1. <u>Either</u> of these cheeses (*is, are*) soft enough to slice. [Which verb agrees with the singular indefinite pronoun *Either*?]

2. <u>Someone</u> usually (*bring, brings*) extra blankets to the stadium on cold nights.

3. <u>Anything</u> Keith suggests (*turn, turns*) out to be a good idea.

4. <u>No one</u> (*plans, plan*) an outdoor party in a thunderstorm!

5. (*Does, Do*) <u>something</u> in the refrigerator smell spoiled?

5e. The following indefinite pronouns are plural:

both	few	many	several

Use a plural verb with these indefinite pronouns when they are used as subjects.

                     S   V

EXAMPLE   **Few** of the birds **have returned** to their nests this spring. [The plural verb phrase *have returned* agrees with the plural subject *Few*. The phrase *of the birds* does not affect agreement, even though it comes between the subject and the verb.]

GO ON ➡

EXERCISE B Circle the verb form in parentheses that agrees with the underlined subject in each of the following sentences.

Example 1. Several of the roses (have, has) budded. [The indefinite pronoun *Several* is plural, so the verb should be plural, too.]

6. A few of the kittens *(has, have)* opened their eyes. [Which verb agrees with the plural indefinite pronoun *few*?]

7. Both of the windows *(was, were)* open in the warm spring weather.

8. Hooray! Several of my drawings *(are, is)* displayed in the school art exhibit!

9. *(Is, Are)* many of the gymnasts training for the state meet?

10. Few from our school *(compete, competes)* every month.

5f. | The following indefinite pronouns may be singular or plural, depending on their meaning in the sentence:

| all | any | more | most | none | some |

Look at the phrase that follows the indefinite pronoun. If the noun in that phrase is singular, the pronoun is also singular. If the noun in that phrase is plural, the pronoun is also plural.

                   V   S

EXAMPLES Was any of the **shipment** damaged? [The subject *any* is singular because it refers to the singular *shipment*. The singular verb *Was* agrees with the singular subject *any*.]

                 V   S

Were any of the **books** damaged? [The subject *any* is plural because it refers to the plural *books*. The plural verb *Were* agrees with the plural subject *any*.]

EXERCISE C Circle the verb form in parentheses that agrees with the underlined subject in each of the following sentences.

Example 1. *(Do, Does)* some of the bread taste stale to you? [The subject is *some*. The noun in the phrase that follows the subject is *bread*, which is singular. The singular verb *Does* agrees with the singular subject.]

11. All of the berries *(has, have)* already been eaten. [Is the noun in the phrase that follows *All* singular or plural? Which verb agrees with the subject?]

12. *(Is, Are)* most of the work completed?

13. None of the runners *(refuse, refuses)* the cool water.

14. Some of my ideas *(is, are)* being considered by the student council.

15. *(Do, Does)* any of the picture appear on the screen?

Pronoun-Antecedent Agreement A

A pronoun is a word that takes the place of a noun or another pronoun. The word a pronoun replaces is called the pronoun's *antecedent*.

5s. A pronoun should agree in number and gender with its antecedent.

Singular pronouns agree with singular antecedents, which may be nouns or other pronouns.

> **EXAMPLE**   When did **Claude Monet** begin **his** waterlily paintings? [The singular pronoun *his* agrees with its singular antecedent, *Claude Monet*.]

Plural pronouns agree with plural antecedents, which may be nouns or other pronouns.

> **EXAMPLE**   The **dogs** looked thirsty, so I gave **them** some water. [The plural pronoun *them* agrees with its plural antecedent, *dogs*.]

Sometimes singular pronouns also show gender. The ***masculine pronouns***—*he, him, his, himself*—refer to males; the ***feminine pronouns***—*she, her, hers, herself*—refer to females; and the ***neuter pronouns***—*it, its, itself*—refer to places, things, ideas, and sometimes to animals. Plural pronouns do not show gender.

> **EXAMPLES**   **Rory** rode **his** new scooter down the sidewalk. [The masculine pronoun *his* agrees with its masculine antecedent, *Rory*.]
>
> Has **Tanya** told you about **her** good news yet? [The feminine pronoun *her* agrees with its feminine antecedent, *Tanya*.]
>
> Give the **cat its** toy. [The neuter pronoun *its* agrees with the antecedent, *cat*, because the gender of the cat is not specified.]
>
> The **teachers** were very proud of **their** students' achievements. [The plural pronoun *their* agrees with its plural antecedent, *teachers*.]

EXERCISE A In each sentence, an antecedent has been underlined for you. On the line provided, write an appropriate pronoun that agrees with the underlined antecedent in number and (where applicable) in gender.

Example 1. Dana turns to ___her___ parents for advice when she has a problem. [The antecedent *Dana* is a singular, feminine antecedent, so the pronoun is singular and feminine.]

1. How sleepy the baby boy looks in _____ car seat!   [Is the antecedent singular or plural? Is the antecedent feminine, masculine, or neuter?]

2. Because the announcers had to refer to players by name, _____ had a list of the players' names handy.

3. Oh, dear—the television has lost _____ picture again.

4. Kathy says that "The Tell-Tale Heart" was _____ favorite short story last year.

5. Do your cats like to have _____ tummies rubbed?

GO ON

5u. | Use a singular pronoun to refer to two or more singular antecedents joined by *or* or *nor*.

> **EXAMPLE** **Louise or Leslie** will bring **her** camcorder. [*Louise* is a singular, feminine antecedent, and *Leslie* is a singular, feminine antecedent. Because they are joined by *or*, they need a singular, feminine pronoun.]

5v. | Use a plural pronoun to refer to two or more antecedents joined by *and*.

> **EXAMPLE** **Jeff and Manuel** forgot **their** jackets. [*Jeff* is a singular, masculine antecedent, and *Manuel* is a singular, masculine antecedent. Because they are joined by *and*, however, they act as a plural antecedent and need a plural pronoun.]

EXERCISE B In each sentence, an antecedent has been underlined for you. On the line provided, write an appropriate pronoun that agrees with the underlined antecedent in number and (where applicable) in gender.

Examples 1. It's time for <u>Andy and his brother</u> to take ___*their*___ pets to the veterinarian. [*Andy* is a singular, masculine antecedent, and so is *brother*. Because they are joined by *and*, however, they act as a plural antecedent and need a plural pronoun.]

   2. Will <u>Mr. Stevens or Mr. Santiago</u> lead ___*his*___ team onto the field first? [*Mr. Stevens* and *Mr. Santiago* are both singular, masculine antecedents. Because they are joined by *or*, they need a singular, masculine pronoun.]

6. The <u>dog and the cat</u> are both due for _____ rabies shots. [Do antecedents joined by *and* take a singular pronoun or a plural pronoun?]

7. Will <u>Andy or his brother</u> take the pets in _____ car? [Do antecedents joined by *or* take a singular or a plural pronoun?]

8. The <u>veterinarian and her assistant</u> will give us _____ advice on pet nutrition.

9. <u>Older dogs and puppies</u> both need exercise. You should walk _____ daily.

10. Will <u>the tag or certificate</u> have the clinic's name on _____?

11. Either <u>Janet or Diane</u> will put the books under _____ desk.

12. Both the <u>dog and the cat</u> have finished _____ dinners.

13. Neither <u>Eileen nor Sharon</u> had _____ library card.

14. <u>Books, folders, and notebooks</u> had _____ own places on the shelf.

15. <u>Sean or Carlos</u> will present _____ project now.

Pronoun-Antecedent Agreement B

5t. Some indefinite pronouns are singular, and some are plural. Other indefinite pronouns can be either singular or plural, depending on their meaning in a sentence.

Singular Indefinite Pronouns

(1) Use a singular pronoun to refer to these indefinite pronouns:

anybody	either	neither	one
anyone	everybody	nobody	somebody
anything	everyone	no one	someone
each	everything	nothing	something

EXAMPLES   **Somebody** will surely volunteer **his or her** time. [*His or her* agrees in number with the antecedent *Somebody* because both are singular. *His or her* agrees in gender because *Somebody* may include both males and females.]

Either of the boys can bring **his** camera. [*His* agrees with the antecedent *Either* in number because both are singular. *His* agrees in gender because the phrase *of the boys* indicates *Either* is masculine.]

EXERCISE A Circle the pronoun or pronoun group in parentheses that agrees with the underlined antecedent in each of the following sentences.

Example 1. Was <u>anyone</u> planning to bring (*his or her*, *their*) bat and ball to practice? [The antecedent *anyone* agrees with *his or her* in number and gender. *Anyone* is always singular and can refer to both males and females.]

1. Far out on the lake, <u>something</u> raised (*their, its*) massive head. [Which pronoun agrees with *something* in number and gender?]

2. <u>Everyone</u> shivered despite (*his or her, their*) coat.

3. Has <u>each</u> of the pandas eaten all (*its, their*) food?

4. <u>One</u> of the girls won first place with (*their, her*) science project.

5. Will <u>somebody</u> please volunteer to present (*their, his or her*) report first?

Plural Indefinite Pronouns

(2) Use a plural pronoun to refer to these indefinite pronouns:

both	few	many	several

EXAMPLE   **Few** of the storm clouds had any lightning in **them.** [The pronoun *them* agrees with the antecedent *Few* because both are plural.]

GO ON

EXERCISE B Circle the pronoun or pronoun group in parentheses that agrees with the underlined antecedent in each of the following sentences.

Example 1. A <u>few</u> of the shoppers consulted the lists (*they*, *he or she*) had brought. [*Few* is always plural, so the pronoun that refers to it should be plural, too.]

6. <u>Several</u> of the store's employees greeted (*their*, *his or her*) customers cheerfully. [Which pronoun agrees with *Several* in number?]

7. Did <u>both</u> of the cashiers get change for (*himself or herself*, *themselves*)?

8. <u>Many</u> of the purchases rang up at (*its*, *their*) discounted prices.

9. Have <u>several</u> of these sweaters already had (*their*, *its*) prices changed?

10. A <u>few</u> of the shoes cannot be sold because (*they*, *it*) are mismatched.

Singular or Plural Indefinite Pronouns

(3) The following indefinite pronouns may be singular or plural, depending on how they are used in a sentence:

all	any	more	most	none	some

Look at the phrase that follows the indefinite pronoun. If the noun in that phrase is singular, the pronoun is also singular. If the noun in that phrase is plural, the pronoun is also plural.

EXAMPLES Has **any** of the novel lived up to **its** reputation? [*Any* is singular because it refers to one novel. The singular pronoun *its* agrees in number with *any*.]

Have **any** of the novels lived up to **their** reputations? [*Any* is plural because it refers to more than one novel. The plural pronoun *their* agrees in number with *any*.]

EXERCISE C Circle the pronoun or pronoun group in parentheses that agrees with the underlined antecedent in each of the following sentences.

Example 1. <u>All</u> of the icy freeway was treacherous. (*It*, *They*) had to be sanded. [*All* is singular because it refers to one freeway. The pronoun that refers to *All* should be singular, too.]

11. <u>Some</u> of the drivers can handle (*their*, *his or her*) cars well on slick roads. [Does *Some* refer to one thing or many?]

12. <u>None</u> of the open streets had much traffic on (*it*, *them*).

13. <u>All</u> of the traffic report was dedicated to announcing road closures. (*They*, *It*) lasted for thirty minutes.

14. Did <u>any</u> of the schools cancel (*their*, *its*) classes?

15. Will <u>most</u> of the ice melt by the afternoon, or will (*it*, *they*) last the entire day?

Principal Parts of Verbs A

Regular Verbs

Every verb has four basic forms, which are called the ***principal parts*** of the verb.

6a. The four principal parts of a verb are the ***base form,*** the ***present participle,*** the ***past,*** and the ***past participle.***

6b. A ***regular verb*** forms its past and past participle by adding *–d* or *–ed* to the base form.

All verbs form the present participle by adding *–ing* to the base form.

BASE FORM	PRESENT PARTICIPLE	PAST	PAST PARTICIPLE
call	[is] calling	called	[have] called
happen	[is] happening	happened	[have] happened
advertise	[is] advertising	advertised	[have] advertised

NOTE The helping verbs *is* and *have* are shown with the present participle and the past participle forms because participles used as verbs always need a helping verb.

EXERCISE A Write the past and the past participle forms of the following verbs.

Example 1. jump ___jumped___ [have] ___jumped___ [*Jump* is a regular verb that adds *–ed* to make its past and past participle forms.]

1. elect _____ [have] _____

[What ending do you add to a regular verb to make its past and past participle forms?]

2. clean _____ [have] _____

3. provide _____ [have] _____

4. play _____ [have] _____

5. gain _____ [have] _____

NOTE When a regular verb ends in silent *–e*, you should add only a *–d* to make its past forms. Also, watch out for common spelling mistakes, such as leaving the *–d* or *–ed* ending off verbs like *biased* (not *bias*) or adding an extra consonant to verbs like *asked* (not *asked*). Remember that verbs often must have the final consonant doubled before you add the ending. If you are unsure of a verb form's spelling, look in a dictionary.

GO ON

EXERCISE B Write the past and the past participle forms of the following verbs.

Example 1. nod ___nodded___ [have] ___nodded___ [*Nod* is a regular verb that adds –*ed* to

make its past forms, but because the vowel sound is short, you must double the *d* before

adding the ending.]

6. grab _____ [have] _____

[What ending do you add to a regular verb to make its past and past participle forms?]

7. suppose _____ [have] _____

8. drown _____ [have] _____

9. prejudice _____ [have] _____

10. use _____ [have] _____

REMINDER When a verb ends in silent –*e*, drop the –*e* before adding the –*ing* ending to make
the present participle form.

       EXAMPLES   care   [is] caring

                     believe   [is] believing

EXERCISE C Write the correct form of the verb on the line provided. Use the verb and the ending given
in the parentheses. Hint: Watch for special spelling situations in which a letter must be dropped or
doubled before the ending is added.

Example 1. (*bud*, present participle form) The apple trees were ___budding___ in the warm spring

weather. [*Bud* is a regular verb that makes its present participle form by adding –*ing*.]

11. (*push*, past form) Yesterday, the first daffodils _____ up through the soil. [Does the verb

have any special spelling concerns? Which ending will make it a past form?]

12. (*practice*, present participle) The older children are already _____ their baseball skills.

13. (*mention*, past form) Just the other day, Hal _____ forming a neighborhood team.

14. (*plant*, past participle) Has your grandmother _____ her spring herbs yet?

15. (*pick*, past participle) Those sparrows have apparently _____ our maple tree for

their nest!

Principal Parts of Verbs B

Irregular Verbs

6c. An *irregular verb* forms its past and past participle in some other way than by adding *–d* or *–ed*.

Irregular verbs often have very different past and past participle forms from regular verbs. However, irregular verbs use the same helping verbs as regular verbs do, and they form the present participle the same way regular verbs do, by adding *–ing*.

NOTE When you are not sure whether a verb is regular or irregular, or what the correct form of an irregular verb is, look up the verb in a dictionary or grammar handbook.

Study the following four ways that irregular verbs change to make their past forms.

1. The verb may make no changes at all.

BASE FORM	PRESENT PARTICIPLE	PAST	PAST PARTICIPLE
cost	[is] costing	cost	[have] cost
put	[is] putting	put	[have] put

EXERCISE A Underline the correct verb form in each sentence.

Example 1. Have you (<u>put</u>, putted) Marco's card in the mail yet? [*Put* is an irregular verb that does not change in its past forms.]

1. Fortunately, none of the house's pipes (*burst, bursted*) during the freeze. [Is the verb *burst* regular or irregular? How does it make its past form?]

2. The plane (*set, setted*) down gently on the runway.

3. The sea gull (*let, letted*) the breeze carry it high into the sky.

4. Has Macie (*hitted, hit*) the bull's-eye more than once?

5. The card only (*cost, costed*) one dollar.

2. The verb's consonants may change.

BASE FORM	PRESENT PARTICIPLE	PAST	PAST PARTICIPLE
spend	[is] spending	spen**t**	[have] spen**t**
make	[is] making	ma**de**	[have] ma**de**

EXERCISE B Underline the correct verb form in each sentence.

Example 1. Have you (<u>sent</u>, sended) Gary an e-mail message today? [*Send* is an irregular verb that makes its past form by changing its final consonant.]

6. The teachers (*spended, spent*) several days preparing this semester's report cards. [Is the verb *spend* regular or irregular? How does it make its past forms?]

GO ON ➡

7. On winter nights we *(heard, heared)* the crackling of icy branches breaking off trees.

8. Jana *(made, maked)* a perfect score on her algebra exam!

9. Have the red wasps *(builded, built)* another nest under the eaves already?

10. The reeds *(bent, bended)* over in the fierce wind.

---

3. A verb's vowel may change.

BASE FORM	PRESENT PARTICIPLE	PAST	PAST PARTICIPLE
ring	[is] ringing	rang	[have] rung
become	[is] becoming	became	[have] become

EXERCISE C Underline the correct verb form in each sentence.

Example 1. Who <u>*(came,* </u> *comed)* to the play? [*Come* is an irregular verb that makes its past form by

changing its vowel.]

11. The car *(ran, runned)* just fine on the way here. [Is the verb *run* irregular or regular? How does it

make its past form?]

12. Was the bear *(stinged, stung)* as it reached for the honey?

13. The runner *(slid, slided)* into home plate.

14. At the watering hole, the antelopes *(drank, drinked)* nervously.

15. Who *(winned, won)* the tournament yesterday?

---

4. A verb may change its vowels and its consonants.

BASE FORM	PRESENT PARTICIPLE	PAST	PAST PARTICIPLE
buy	[is] buying	**bought**	[have] **bought**
stand	[is] standing	st**ood**	[have] st**ood**

EXERCISE D Underline the correct verb form in each sentence.

Example 1. What decorations has Marie <u>*(bought,* </u> *buyed)* for the party? [*Buy* is an irregular verb

that makes its past forms by changing vowels and consonants.]

16. The prairie dog *(seeked, sought)* the safety of its burrow. [Is the verb *seek* regular or irregular?]

17. The temperature had *(goed, gone)* from 72°F to 36°F by the time the cold front blew through.

18. How tall you have *(grown, growed)* since I last saw you!

19. The gerbil *(tore, teared)* the newspaper into small strips for its nest.

20. The committee has *(written, writed)* its decision on the matter.

Tense

| **6d.** | The *tense* of a verb indicates the time of the action or of the state of being expressed by the verb. |

The time of an action or state of being can be *past, present,* or *future.* Each verb has six tenses. The six tenses express time in different ways.

Here are three of the tenses.

PRESENT The oak tree **shades** the trail. [The present tense verb *shades* describes an action happening now. Present verbs describe something that is happening or existing now.]

PAST The oak tree **shaded** the trail. [The past tense verb *shaded* describes an action happening in the past. Past verbs describe something happening or existing in the past.]

FUTURE The oak tree **will shade** the trail. [The future tense verb *will shade* describes an action that will happen at some time in the future. Future verbs describe something happening or existing in the future. Notice that the future tense always uses *will* or *shall* as a helping verb.]

EXERCISE A Identify the tense of the underlined verb in each of the following sentences. Write *present, past,* or *future* on the line provided.

Example _past_ **1.** The silvery balloon <u>reflected</u> the child's smile. [The verb *reflected* describes an action that took place in the past.]

_____ **1.** The boys <u>will ride</u> the Ferris wheel later. [In what time frame is the action described by the verb phrase *will ride* occurring?]

_____ **2.** <u>Are</u> they old enough to go in the fun house?

_____ **3.** How confusing the house of mirrors <u>was</u>!

_____ **4.** We all <u>ate</u> roasted corn on the cob.

_____ **5.** Next year, the fair <u>will come</u> to town in May.

Here are three more of the six tenses. These tenses are called the *perfect tenses.* They describe action that is complete, or "perfect."

PRESENT PERFECT The oak tree **has shaded** the trail for an hour. [The present perfect tense verb *has shaded* describes an action that is complete at the present moment.]

PAST PERFECT By the time the sun was high, the oak tree **had shaded** the trail for an hour. [The past perfect tense verb *had shaded* describes an action that was completed before a specific time in the past.]

FUTURE PERFECT By the time the sun is high, the oak tree **will have shaded** the trail for an hour. [The future perfect tense verb *will have shaded* describes an action that will be completed before a specific time in the future.]

GO ON

TIP Notice that the perfect tenses always use a form of *have* as a helping verb. Remember that the first helping verb in a verb phrase should agree in number with the subject.

> **EXAMPLES** The oak **tree has** shaded the trail for an hour. [The singular helping verb
> *has* agrees with the singular subject *tree*.]
> The oak **trees have** shaded the trail for an hour. [The plural helping verb
> *have* agrees with the plural subject *trees*.]

EXERCISE B Identify the tense of the underlined verb in each of the following sentences. Write *present perfect, past perfect,* or *future perfect* on the line provided.

Example __present perfect__ **1.** Have you ever <u>dialed</u> a wrong number? [The action in the

sentence was completed at some point before now.]

_____ **6.** The caller said, "<u>Have</u> I <u>reached</u> the pizza delivery place?" [Was the action

in the sentence completed in the past, or will it occur in the future?]

_____ **7.** "No," I answered, "I <u>have</u> never <u>sold</u> a pizza in my life."

_____ **8.** I wasn't angry, because I <u>had had</u> the same problem the day before.

_____ **9.** My best friend's family <u>had changed</u> their phone number.

_____**10.** By tomorrow, I <u>will have found</u> out the new number.

EXERCISE C In each of the following sentences, write the form of the verb described in parentheses. Write your answer on the line provided.

Example 1. Which candidate _____have_____ the students _____elected_____ class president?

(present perfect tense of *elect*) [The present perfect tense is formed with the helping

verb *have* and the past participle form of the verb.]

11. Nina _____ a funny story about herself. (past tense of *write*) [How is the past tense

of a verb formed?]

12. Our father _____ four tickets to the play. (past perfect tense of *buy*)

13. Jason _____ always _____ that Phoenix was a beautiful city. (present

perfect tense of *think*)

14. Teresa and her sister _____ painting the set before the next rehearsal. (future tense

of *finish*)

15. I _____ a lot about fly-fishing from my aunt. (present perfect tense of *learn*)

Third Course

Progressive Forms

Each of the six tenses can also describe an action or state of being that is in progress. These forms of the six tenses are called the ***progressive forms.*** Here are three of the progressive forms of verbs. Notice that the progressive forms of tenses always use a form of *be* as a helping verb.

PRESENT PROGRESSIVE	Leo **is setting** up the computer now. [The present progressive verb *is setting* expresses an action that is in progress now.]
PAST PROGRESSIVE	Yesterday, Leo **was setting** up the computer. [The past progressive verb *was setting* expresses an action that was in progress in the past.]
FUTURE PROGRESSIVE	Leo **will be setting** up the computer tomorrow. [The future progressive verb *will be setting* expresses an action that will be in progress in the future.]

EXERCISE A Identify the tense of the underlined verb in each of the following sentences. Write *present progressive, past progressive,* or *future progressive* on the line provided.

Example ___*present progressive*___ **1.** Are the puppies <u>tumbling</u> around on the floor? [The action is in progress in the present.]

_____ **1.** <u>Will</u> you <u>be singing</u> at your uncle's wedding? [Is the action in progress in the past, the present, or the future?]

_____ **2.** Fish <u>were jumping</u> to catch insects.

_____ **3.** Hold on—I <u>am having</u> trouble with the camera's flash.

_____ **4.** <u>Were</u> the gardeners <u>watering</u> the plants?

_____ **5.** Are you <u>feeling</u> stronger since you began jogging?

The three perfect tenses also have progressive forms. The progressive forms of the perfect tenses express action or state of being that was or will be in progress and has been or will be complete in the present, the past, or the future.

PRESENT PERFECT PROGRESSIVE	Leo **has been setting** up the computer all morning. [The present perfect progressive verb *has been setting* expresses an action that has been in progress but is complete now.]
PAST PERFECT PROGRESSIVE	Before he took a break, Leo **had been setting** up the computer for an hour. [The past perfect progressive verb *had been setting* expresses an action that was in progress but was completed in the past.]
FUTURE PERFECT PROGRESSIVE	By noon, Leo **will have been setting** up the computer for two hours. [The future perfect progressive verb *will have been setting* expresses an action that will be in progress but will be completed in the future.]

GO ON ▶

EXERCISE B Identify the tense of the underlined verb in each of the following sentences. Write *present perfect progressive, past perfect progressive,* or *future perfect progressive* on the line provided.

Example ___present perfect progressive___ **1.** Have you <u>been writing</u> in your journal? [The action is in progress in the present.]

_____ **6.** For how many days <u>has</u> it <u>been snowing</u>? [Is the action in progress in the past, the present, or the future?]

_____ **7.** Squirrels <u>had been stealing</u> food from the bird feeder.

_____ **8.** These ducks <u>have been migrating</u> to this location for many years.

_____ **9.** By Friday, the runners <u>will have been training</u> for two weeks.

_____ **10.** The old-fashioned train <u>had been making</u> the same trip over and over.

The six verb tenses and their progressive forms help the reader understand when events take place. The tenses and forms can also be used together to show in what order a sequence of events takes place.

> **EXAMPLES** The test **was** not difficult. [The past tense verb *was* shows that this occurred in the past.]
>
> The test **was** not as difficult as we **had expected.** [Both of these occurred in the past. First, we *had expected*. Then, the test *was*.]

EXERCISE C In each of the following sentences, write the form of the verb described in parentheses. Write your answer on the line provided.

Example 1. _____Have_____ you ever _____written_____ an entire book? (present perfect tense of *write*) [What helping verb is used with the present perfect tense?]

11. Mr. Diaz told us that he _____ his manuscript to the publisher. (past perfect tense of *send*) [What helping verb is used with the past perfect tense?]

12. He _____ something from his publisher by March. (future perfect tense of *hear*)

13. Many people _____ books that will never be published. (present perfect tense of *write*)

14. Other writers _____ him how difficult it was to get published. (present perfect progressive tense of *tell*)

15. In spite of many disappointments, he _____ he will keep working to see his words in print. (past tense of *say*)

Consistency of Tense

6f. Do not change needlessly from one tense to another.

When you describe events that happened in the same time frame, use the same tense in all your verbs. For instance, if you are telling a story that happened in the past, narrate each event using past tense verbs. If you change from one tense to another, the reader may become confused about the order of the events.

INCONSISTENT	When I first saw the bike, I knew I had to have it. It was perfect! It has every accessory I want. I worked for two months to earn money. I deliver papers, mow lawns, and do odd jobs for neighbors. Finally, I will earn enough money. Dad is driving me to the store, and I buy the bike with my own hard-earned cash! [Do the actions take place in the past, the present, or the future?]
CONSISTENT	When I first saw the bike, I knew I had to have it. It was perfect! It had every accessory I wanted. I worked for two months to earn money. I was delivering papers, mowing lawns, and doing odd jobs for neighbors. Finally, I had earned enough money. Dad drove me to the store, and I bought the bike with my own hard-earned cash! [All the verbs are in the past tense or the past perfect tense. The actions clearly took place in the past.]

EXERCISE A Read each sentence, paying special attention to the underlined verbs. If the verbs' tenses are consistent, write **C** on the line provided. If the verbs' tenses are inconsistent, write **I** on the line.

Examples ___C___ **1.** That athlete runs fast and wins the race almost every time. [The verb *runs* and the verb *wins* both describe action that occurs in the present, so the tense is consistent.]

___I___ **2.** The glass of water sat in the sun and heats up. [The verb *sat* describes action that occurred in the past, but the verb *heats* describes action that occurs in the present, so the verbs' tenses are not consistent.]

_____ **1.** The beavers have built a new dam and make a nest in it. [Is the action of *have built* occurring in the past, the present, or the future? Is the action of *make* in the same time frame?]

_____ **2.** The car handles well and gets good gas mileage.

_____ **3.** The crane will lift the beam up and lowered it onto the structure.

_____ **4.** Juanita put a CD in the player and adjusts the volume.

_____ **5.** Is the traffic bad at this time of day, and are there any construction delays?

_____ **6.** Each student will have taken notes and listens to the guest speaker.

_____ **7.** Turn into the lot and choose a parking space.

_____ **8.** Because they studied hard, they did well on the test.

GO ON ➡

_____ **9.** Pigeons <u>clustered</u> on the roof and occasionally <u>flutter</u> down to the ground.

_____ **10.** We <u>will brush</u> our teeth and <u>have gone</u> to the dentist.

> **REMINDER** Sometimes, people narrate a past event in the present tense. This makes the event come alive, as if it were happening right now. When you choose to narrate an event in the present tense, be consistent. Do not switch between present and past unnecessarily.

EXERCISE B Each of the sentences below is inconsistent in its tense. Rewrite the sentence so that the tense is consistent.

Example 1. The computer <u>froze</u> up, and my document <u>disappears</u> into cyberspace. [In this sentence, *froze* describes an action that happened in the past, but *disappears* describes an action happening in the present. The sentence would make more sense if both verbs described actions that happened in the past. However, both actions could occur in the present or even in the future, as long as the tenses are consistent.]

The computer froze up, and my document disappeared into cyberspace.

11. The haze <u>clears</u> away, and the day <u>was</u> beautiful. [What time frame does the first verb describe? What time frame does the second verb describe? What consistent time frame would make the most sense?]

_____

_____

12. The student council <u>will vote</u> and <u>chose</u> a location for the class picnic.

_____

_____

13. A pair of kingfishers <u>hunt</u> for fish while we <u>watched</u>.

_____

_____

14. The wind <u>blows</u> through the trees, and leaves <u>fell</u> to the ground.

_____

_____

15. When <u>will</u> the computer store <u>hold</u> its grand opening and <u>allowed</u> customers to come in?

_____

Active and Passive Voice

6g. A verb in the *active voice* expresses an action done by its subject. A verb in the *passive voice* expresses an action done to its subject.

> ACTIVE   The amusement park **offered** me a free ticket. [The action of the verb *offered* was done by the subject *park*.]
>
> PASSIVE   A free ticket **was offered** to me by the amusement park. [The action of the verb *was offered* was done to the subject *ticket*.]

EXERCISE A   Read each sentence below, paying special attention to the underlined verb. If the sentence is in the active voice, write *AV* on the line provided. Write *PV* if the sentence is in the passive voice.

Examples __PV__ **1.** The corn <u>was harvested</u> in just one week. [The action of the verb *was harvested* was done to the subject *corn*.]

__AV__ **2.** The melting ice <u>swelled</u> the river to its banks. [The action of the verb *swelled* was done by the subject *ice*.]

_____ **1.** Mom <u>gave</u> me a ride to soccer practice. [Is the subject *Mom* acting in the sentence or being acted on?]

_____ **2.** The dog <u>was scolded</u> for chewing up a book. [Is the subject *dog* acting in the sentence or being acted on?]

_____ **3.** Who <u>changed</u> the station on my radio?

_____ **4.** The certificate read, "You <u>are appreciated</u>!"

_____ **5.** The cashier <u>counts</u> out the change correctly.

_____ **6.** Every bill <u>is counted</u> separately.

_____ **7.** Was the choir <u>singing</u> the school song?

_____ **8.** Has the mechanic <u>changed</u> the transmission fluid yet?

_____ **9.** <u>Take</u> out this bag of trash, please.

_____ **10.** Will the game <u>be announced</u> by the school's regular announcer?

GO ON

Developmental Language Skills

79

Passive voice is as correct as active voice, but passive voice often slows down the pace of writing and speaking. Active voice is more direct; passive voice is wordier. You may want to rewrite passive sentences, putting them in the active voice.

The passive voice is useful when you do not know or do not want to reveal the performer of the action, or when you want to emphasize the receiver of the action.

> **EXAMPLES** Overnight, the sidewalk was cleaned. [The performer of the action *was cleaned* is not known.]
>
> A collection of books has been given to the library. [The performer of the action *has been given* is not revealed.]
>
> The nests had been built by robins. [*Nests* is the receiver of the action *had been built*. Moving *nests* to the front of the sentence gives them emphasis.]

EXERCISE B Each of the sentences below is written in passive voice. Rewrite each sentence so that it is in active voice. If the sentence should remain in the passive voice, write *C* on the line and explain why the passive voice is needed.

Example 1. The garden was weeded by my grandmother. [*My grandmother* is performing the action *was weeded,* so she should be the subject of the sentence.]

_My grandmother weeded the garden._____

11. The ball was caught by the receiver. [Who performs the action *was caught*? Make that person or thing the subject, and rewrite the sentence so that the subject is acting on the ball.]

_____

12. The walls are painted by Mom and Dad.

_____

13. Will the phone be answered by you?

_____

14. The book has already been checked out.

_____

15. A cold was caught by my big sister.

_____

Lie and *Lay*, *Sit* and *Set*, *Rise* and *Raise*

6h. The verb *lie* means "to rest," "to recline," or "to remain in a lying position." *Lie* does not take an object. The verb *lay* means "to put" or "to place (something somewhere)." *Lay* generally takes an object.

BASE FORM	PRESENT PARTICIPLE	PAST	PAST PARTICIPLE
lie	[is] lying	lay	[have] lain
lay	[is] laying	laid	[have] laid

EXAMPLES   **Lay** your heavy book bag under the desk. [*Lay* means "to put." The verb takes an object, *bag*.]

The book bag **lay** under the desk. [*Lay* is the past form of *lie* and means "to recline." It does not take an object.]

REMINDER When we say that a verb takes an object, we mean that the verb tells of an action directed toward a person, place, or thing. In the sentence, "Matt lobbed the ball over the net," the action of lobbing is directed at the ball. The ball is what gets lobbed.

TIP The verb *lie* can also mean "to tell an untruth." When you use this meaning of *lie*, it is a regular verb *(lie, lied, have lied.)*

EXERCISE A Underline the correct verb in the following sentences.

Example 1. The valley (<u>lay</u>, laid) between the river and the hills. [The verb means "to rest" or "to recline," so *lay*, the past form of *lie*, is the correct verb.]

1. Julie (*lay, laid*) the poster across the desk. [Does the verb mean "to rest" or "to put"?]

2. When the kitten is tired, it will (*lie, lay*) down and nap.

3. Silence (*lay, laid*) over the houses and shops as the night slipped away.

4. Have you (*laid, lain*) out the clothes you want to pack?

5. The carpenters will (*lay, lie*) the new floor after the walls are painted.

6i. The verb *sit* means "to rest in an upright, seated position." *Sit* seldom takes an object. The verb *set* means "to put" or "to place (something somewhere)." *Set* generally takes an object.

BASE FORM	PRESENT PARTICIPLE	PAST	PAST PARTICIPLE
sit	[is] sitting	sat	[have] sat
set	[is] setting	set	[have] set

EXAMPLES   **Is** Diego **sitting** in front of the house? [The verb in this sentence means "to rest in an upright, seated position."]

Set the book down, and come look out the window! [The verb in this sentence means "to put."]

GO ON

EXERCISE B Underline the correct verb in each of the following sentences.

Example 1. The hikers (set, sat) their packs on the boulders and drank from their water bottles.

[In this sentence, the verb means "to put," so *set* is the correct verb.]

6. The cook *(sat, set)* the vegetables in the pan. [Is something being placed somewhere, or is

someone or something resting in an upright, seated position?]

7. Are my keys *(sitting, setting)* on the kitchen counter?

8. The passengers had just *(sat, set)* down and fastened their seatbelts.

9. Please *(set, sit)* that photograph back on the shelf.

10. *(Setting, Sitting)* on the patio are the new plant cuttings.

6j. The verb *rise* means "to go in an upward direction." *Rise* does not take an object. The verb *raise* means "to move (something) in an upward direction." *Raise* generally takes an object.

BASE FORM	PRESENT PARTICIPLE	PAST	PAST PARTICIPLE
rise	[is] rising	rose	[have] risen
raise	[is] raising	raised	[have] raised

EXAMPLES The child **raised** the cup of juice and took a drink. [In this sentence, something—a cup—is being lifted by someone—the child. The verb takes an object.]

The child **rose** from her seat and asked for some juice. [In this sentence, no one is lifting anything up. Instead, the child is moving in an upward direction. The verb does not take an object.]

EXERCISE C Underline the correct verb in each of the following sentences. Hint: If you choose a form of the verb *raise,* be sure that you can find the thing in the sentence that is being *raised* (the object).

Example 1. Please *(raise, rise)* the blinds and open the windows. [In this sentence, something—

the blinds—is being lifted. The verb takes an object, so *raise* is the correct verb.]

11. Who will *(raise, rise)* his or her hand and start the discussion? [Is something being lifted by

someone, or is upward motion being described?]

12. The helicopter was *(raising, rising)* into the sky.

13. The concertgoers *(rose, raised)* to their feet and applauded.

14. Before the sun had *(risen, rose)*, we packed up the campsite and drove off.

15. Tie the balloon firmly, or it will *(rise, raise)* all the way to the ceiling.

The Nominative Case

Case is the form that a noun or pronoun takes to show its relationship to other words in a sentence. In English, there are three cases: nominative, objective, and possessive.

Subjects

7b.   The *subject* of a verb should be in the nominative case.

The subject of a verb is the person, place, thing, or idea that performs the action of that verb. The nominative pronouns—*I, you, he, she, it, we,* and *they*—are used as subjects.

> **EXAMPLES**   **Martha** says that **they** can go to the movies. [*Martha* is the subject of the verb *says,* and *they* is the subject of the verb phrase *can go.*]
>
> Should **you** and **I** go as well? [*You* and *I* are both subjects of the verb phrase *should go.*]

EXERCISE A   Read each sentence, and then underline the correct pronoun in parentheses. Each sentence uses the pronoun as a subject, so the pronoun should be in the nominative case.

Example 1.   Did (they, them) build that new fence?   [The pronoun is the subject of the verb *Did build.*

The pronoun *they* is in the nominative case.]

1. Tomorrow *(they, them)* will sign up for guitar lessons.   [Is the pronoun acting as a subject? Which case form is required?]

2. Has *(he, him)* finished reading the novel yet?

3. *(Them, They)* do all the annoying chores around here.

4. *(We, Us)* can't wait for the harvest to begin!

5. Was *(her, she)* here first, or were you?

Predicate Nominatives

7c.   A *predicate nominative* should also be in the nominative case.

You may remember that a predicate nominative is a word or group of words that is in the predicate and that renames the subject of the verb. A predicate nominative completes the meaning of a linking verb. Common linking verbs are *is, were, be, are,* and *seems.*

>   S   LV   PN
> **EXAMPLES**   This mountain range is an ancient **landform.** [The subject is *mountain range,* and the word *landform* renames *mountain range.* The word *ancient* tells what kind of landform. The subject and the predicate nominative are linked by the verb *is.*]
>
>   S   LV PN   PN
> The most talented singers are **he** and **you.** [*Singers* is the sentence's subject, and the linking verb *are* links the subject to the predicate nominative. *He* and *you* are in the nominative case.]

GO ON ▶

> **TIP** When you are not sure which pronoun to use for a predicate nominative, follow these
> steps: Put the subject in the predicate nominative's place and the predicate nominative in
> the subject's place. Ask yourself, "Which pronoun sounds better in the subject's place?"
> Rewrite the sentence, using the nominative pronoun form as the predicate nominative.
>
>   **EXAMPLE** The strongest man is *(he, him)*. [Which sounds better—*He is the strongest*
>   *man* or *Him is the strongest man*? The pronoun *He* sounds better.]
> **FINAL SENTENCE** The strongest man is **he.** [*He* is the nominative form and should be used
>   as the predicate nominative.]

EXERCISE B Underline the correct pronoun in each sentence. Each pronoun is in the predicate and
should be in the nominative case.

Example 1. The champions were *(they, them)*. [The pronoun is a predicate nominative, so the

                nominative case form *they* is needed.]

6. No, the driver was not *(he, him)*. [Does the pronoun complete the linking verb *was*?]

7. Will the reader be *(she, her)*?

8. The gymnast was certainly not *(me, I)*.

9. What marvelous friends are *(them, they)*!

10. The one who is athletic is *(he, him)*.

> **TIP** To find out which pronoun to use in a compound subject or predicate nominative, try the
> pronoun by itself with the verb.
>   **S**   **S**   **V**
>   **EXAMPLE** *(Him, He)* and **Gloria** attend college. [Which sounds better—***Him** attends*
>   *college* or ***He** attends college*? The pronoun *He* sounds better with the verb
>   *attends*.]
>   **S**   **S**   **V**
> **FINAL SENTENCE** **He** and **Gloria** attend college. [*He* is the nominative pronoun and should
>   be used in this compound subject.]

EXERCISE C Underline the correct pronoun in each sentence.

Example 1. Will Lee and *(they, them)* visit next week? [*They will visit* sounds better.]

11. Throughout the soccer game, the most dedicated players were Ted and *(we, us)*. [Which sounds

      better—*We were the players* or *Us were the players*?]

12. You and *(I, me)* need to talk.

13. The winners of the science fair were Dora and *(him, he)*!

14. Where did Max and *(them, they)* go after their exam was over?

15. Tim and *(she, her)* often help my parents in the garden.

The Objective Case

Objective case pronouns—*me, you, him, her, it, us,* and *them*—are used as direct objects, indirect objects, and objects of prepositions.

Direct Objects

7d.	A direct object should be in the objective case.

A direct object is a noun, pronoun, or word group that receives the action of a verb.

                                               S   V   DO

EXAMPLES   The flames burned too high, so the cook turned **them** down. [What were turned down? *Them* (the flames) were turned down.]

                                    S   V   DO   DO

The reading quiz caught **them** and **us** off guard. [Who were caught off guard? *Them* and *us* are both direct objects of the verb *caught.* More than one pronoun may be the direct object of the verb. Be sure that both pronouns are in the objective case.]

EXERCISE A Underline the correct pronoun in parentheses in each item. In each item, the italicized pronoun is the direct object of the verb and needs to be in the objective case.

Example 1. Jack told *(him, he)* about our plans. [The pronoun is the direct object of the verb *told,* so you should use *him,* the objective case form.]

1. Mr. Dell will meet *(us, we)* at the trailhead on Saturday morning. [Which pronoun is in objective case form—*us* or *we?*]

2. Charla will help lead our group. Who will give *(she, her)* one of the maps?

3. Did you mark the trails clearly? Yes, I marked *(they, them)* all.

4. Before we split up, tell *(we, us)* which trail to follow.

5. Will you meet *(me, I)* where these two trails come together?

Indirect Objects

7e.	An indirect object should also be in the objective case.

As you know, an indirect object tells *to whom, to what, for whom,* or *for what* the action of the verb was done. When you see a sentence with an indirect object, you will find a direct object as well.

                                   S   V   IO   DO

EXAMPLES   Aunt Sue baked **us** some bread. [For whom was the bread baked? It was baked for us, so *us* is the indirect object of *baked.*]

                                     V   IO   DO

Please send **them** the invitation. [To whom will the invitation be sent? It will be sent to them, so *them* is the indirect object of *send.* The subject is understood to be *You.*]

GO ON

EXERCISE B Underline the correct pronoun in each sentence. Each pronoun acts as an indirect object of a verb, so be sure to use the objective case form.

Example 1. Will the coach bring *(we, us)* the new softball uniforms soon? [The verb *bring* takes

uniforms as its direct object, and the indirect object is *us*. Any kind of object requires the

objective case form of the pronoun, so *us* is correct.]

6. Show *(I, me)* a photo of the uniforms in that catalog, please. [Is the pronoun an object of the

verb *Show*? Which is in the objective case—*I* or *me*?]

7. Coach Sanchez gave *(us, we)* the chance to choose the numbers on our jerseys.

8. Could you hand *(him, he)* a list of players on the team?

9. Have you told *(they, them)* the good news about Tanya?

10. Yes, the coach just offered *(her, she)* a spot on the team!

Objects of Prepositions

7f.   An object of a preposition should be in the objective case.

As you may know, an object of a preposition is the noun or pronoun that follows any
preposition.

                                              P OP
EXAMPLES   Please give these copies **to her.** [The preposition *to* is followed by the
                  object pronoun *her.*]
                            P   OP
                  After them, may we use that basketball? [The preposition *After* is followed
                  by the object pronoun *them.*]

NOTE▶ When two or more pronouns follow a preposition, each pronoun must be in the objective
case: "just between **them** and **me.**"

EXERCISE C Underline the correct pronoun in each sentence. The pronoun will always be the object of a
preposition and will require the objective case form.

Example 1. Set my lunch down beside *(her, she)*, please. [The word that follows the preposition

beside is its object and must be in objective case form.]

11. Kindly do not splash water on *(me, I)*! [Find the preposition. Which word follows it? Is that word

in objective case form?]

12. The songs had us dancing as we sang along with *(they, them)*.

13. Let's organize this information so that it makes sense to *(him and her, he and she)*.

14. Our family dined with *(they, them)* last night.

15. Why don't you stand between *(him and me, he and I)* for this picture?

Special Problems in Pronoun Usage
Who and *Whom*

7h. The use of *who* or *whom* in a subordinate clause depends on how the pronoun functions in the clause.

Who and *whoever* are nominative case pronouns. Use them as subjects of sentences and as predicate nominatives. *Whom* and *whomever* are objective case pronouns. Use them as direct objects, indirect objects, or objects of prepositions.

NOMINATIVE **Who** will plant that tree this weekend? [The subject of the sentence, performing the action, is *Who*.]

The winner of the math contest was **who**? [The predicate nominative, which renames the subject, is *who*.]

OBJECTIVE For **whom** are we waiting? [*Whom* is the object of the preposition *For*.]

Whom did Evan call? [*Whom* is the direct object of the verb phrase *did call*.]

Sometimes, the words *who, whom, whoever,* and *whomever* are used at the beginning of subordinate clauses. (As you may remember, a subordinate clause has a subject and verb, but the clause does not express a complete thought. It is part of a larger sentence.)

EXAMPLES I wonder **who** will work on the project. [The underlined subordinate clause uses *who* as a subject, so the nominative case form is needed.]

Here is a speaker **whom** listeners always enjoy. [The underlined subordinate clause uses *whom* as a direct object of the verb *enjoy*, so the objective case form is needed.]

EXERCISE A Circle the correct form of the pronoun in each sentence below. First, decide how the pronoun functions in the underlined clause.

Example 1. Did you find out (*who,* (*whom*)) the students elected? [In the clause, the pronoun acts as the direct object of the verb *elected*. Object pronouns use the objective case form.]

1. The athletes (*who, whom*) I most admire are strong and intelligent. [Is the pronoun the subject or an object of a verb or preposition?]

2. (*Who, Whom*) went with you to the concert? [Is the pronoun the subject or an object of a verb or preposition?]

3. Please tell (*whoever, whomever*) shows up that the meeting has been cancelled.

4. (*Who, Whom*) will teach your algebra class next year?

5. I called my friend Jenna, (*who, whom*) I haven't seen in a year.

6. The best man in the wedding is the one (*who, whom*) is wearing a white rose.

7. To (*who, whom*) are these flowers being sent?

8. Guess (*who, whom*) is at the door!

9. My great-grandfather, about *(who, whom)* I have often spoken, was born in Africa.

10. The prize will be given to *(whoever, whomever)* the judges choose.

Appositives

| **7i.** | A pronoun used as an appositive is in the same case as the word to which it refers. |

An appositive, as you may remember, is a noun or pronoun placed beside another noun or pronoun to identify or describe it.

NOUN APPOSITIVE   Maya's sister **Dena** takes violin lessons. [The noun *Dena* identifies *sister.*]

PRONOUN APPOSITIVE   The speakers, **he** and **they,** kept the audience entertained. [The pronouns *he* and *they* identify *speakers.*]

Sometimes, a pronoun is followed by an appositive that identifies the pronoun.

EXAMPLES   **We** violinists must practice every day. [*We*, the subject pronoun, is identified by the appositive *violinists.* Because *We* is the subject of the sentence, it is in the nominative case.]

Give **us** young musicians credit for being determined! [*Us*, the object of *Give*, is identified as *young musicians* by the appositive.]

TIP Whether a pronoun acts as an appositive or comes right before an appositive, the key is to make sure that both the pronoun and the noun are in the same case. If you are not sure which pronoun form to use, remove the noun and complete the sentence correctly without it.

STEP 1   *(We, Us)* violinists love to play. [Now, remove the appositive, *violinists.*]

STEP 2   *(We, Us)* love to play. [Which pronoun sounds correct?]

STEP 3   **We** violinists love to play.

EXERCISE B Underline the correct pronoun in each sentence below. If you are not sure what case the pronoun should take, use the previous steps to help you decide.

Example 1. (*Us*, We) students took a tour of the radio station. [The pronoun serves as the subject of the verb *took* and should be in the nominative case. The noun *students* renames the pronoun. *We* is correct.]

11. Everyone—the teachers and *(we, us)*—visited the radio station this morning. [Is the pronoun the appositive of a subject or an object?]

12. The funny radio hosts especially entertained the teachers, Mr. Holland and *(she, her).*

13. Even so, the many buttons in the control room impressed *(us, we)* all.

14. *(We, Us)* visitors had to stay quiet while the show was being recorded.

15. Remind me to thank the hosts, Karl and *(she, her),* for letting us visit the station.

Clear Reference A

7k. A pronoun should refer clearly to its antecedent.

You may remember that the word or word group that a pronoun stands for is called its antecedent. In clear writing, readers can find the antecedent of each pronoun and are able to understand each pronoun's meaning. A pronoun should clearly refer to its antecedent.

EXAMPLE The couple received a gift. **They** opened **it.** [The antecedent of *They* is *couple*, and the antecedent of *it* is *gift*.]

One problem with pronoun reference is ***ambiguous reference.*** This problem occurs when any one of two or more words can be a pronoun's antecedent. As you can see, there are several ways to revise a sentence that has an ambiguous pronoun.

AMBIGUOUS Mark laughed with Joshua when he told that joke. [The pronoun *he* could refer to *Joshua* or *Mark*. The sentence leaves readers wondering which person is the antecedent.]

CLEAR When Mark told that joke, **he** laughed with Joshua. [In this revision, the pronoun *he* clearly refers to *Mark.*]

CLEAR Mark laughed with Joshua when **Joshua** told that joke. [Sometimes, you can make a pronoun error clear by replacing the pronoun with a noun. Just make sure that your writing does not sound unnecessarily repetitive when you make such a replacement.]

EXERCISE A Read each sentence. Then, decide if the underlined pronoun refers clearly to one antecedent or refers ambiguously to more than one antecedent. If the pronoun reference is clear, write **C** on the line before the sentence. If the pronoun reference is ambiguous, write **A** on the line. Hint: Draw an arrow from the pronoun to its antecedent. If you can draw only one arrow, the pronoun reference is clear. If you can draw more than one arrow, the pronoun reference is ambiguous.

Examples ___A___ **1.** Sarah talked to Mother about her new job. [In this sentence, the pronoun *her* could refer to Sarah or to Mother. It is hard to tell whose new job is being discussed. The pronoun reference is ambiguous.]

___C___ **2.** The father rocked the baby until she fell asleep. [In this sentence, the pronoun *she* must refer to the baby since a father is male, not female. The pronoun reference is clear.]

_____ **1.** After the boys talked to the coach, he advised them to run some wind sprints. [Could *he* possibly refer to more than one word or word group, or is the reference clear?]

_____ **2.** My uncle asked his son to bring his snow boots inside. [Could *his* possibly refer to more than one word or word group, or is the reference clear?]

_____ **3.** Zach let Brian know that his backpack was out in the hall.

`GO ON`

_____ **4.** Have the girls taken the puppies to their home yet?

_____ **5.** Make sure that Carrie knows her lines and that Jason has his costume ready.

_____ **6.** The ship rolled on the wave as it ran across the ocean.

_____ **7.** After Sonia finished her solo, the crowd cheered.

_____ **8.** Margaret e-mailed her aunt about her recipe for pasta salad.

_____ **9.** Did the artists or the viewers say that they enjoyed the exhibit?

_____ **10.** Is Mars the brightest planet this month, or is it Venus?

EXERCISE B Fix the unclear pronoun reference in each sentence below by rewriting each sentence on the line provided. The unclear pronoun has been underlined for you.

Example 1. The outdoor theater has great lighting and a large stage, but it is the band's favorite

feature. [The word *it* does not clearly refer to the stage or the lighting, so *it* has been

replaced with a more specific reference, *the stage*.]

The outdoor theater has great lighting and a large stage, but the stage is the band's

favorite feature.

11. After Billy and José left band practice, he realized he'd left his notebook behind. [Could *he* possibly refer to more than one word or word group, or is the reference clear?]

_____

12. The helicopter created a small dust cloud, and I enjoyed watching it.

_____

13. While Doug and Terrell were at the airport, he ran into a friend from elementary school.

_____

14. The day after she bought the blue skirt and the yellow dress, Tisha wore it to school.

_____

15. As Mr. Moreno and Mrs. Burke presented an award to the soccer team, they had smiles on their faces.

_____

Third Course

Clear Reference B

7k. | A pronoun should refer clearly to its antecedent.

One problem with pronoun reference is *general reference.* This problem occurs when a writer uses a pronoun that refers to a general idea rather than to a specific antecedent. Writers are most likely to slip into general reference when they use words like *it, that, this, such,* and *which.* These words may be easy to understand in speech, but they can be misinterpreted in unclear writing.

> **GENERAL** Dawn has a math test to study for, a science project to complete, and a solo to memorize, but it shouldn't be a problem.   [The pronoun *it* in this sentence could refer to any of these three types of homework. On the other hand, *it* could refer to the problem of too much homework. Readers cannot tell for certain. The writer should avoid this general reference.]
>
> **CLEAR** Dawn has a math test to study for, a science project to complete, and a solo to memorize, but **completing these assignments** shouldn't be a problem. [In this sentence, the writer uses exact language and avoids general reference.]
>
> **GENERAL** The phone was ringing, and someone was at the door, **which** caught me off guard. [The relative pronoun *which* seems to refer to the combination of demands on the writer, but it is hard to know for certain. *Which* is used as a general reference that the writer should avoid.]
>
> **CLEAR** The phone was ringing, and someone was at the door. **These demands** caught me off guard. [The word group *These demands* is clearer and more exact than *which.*]

EXERCISE A Read each pair of sentences. Write **C** on the blank before each sentence that uses clear reference and **G** on the blank before each sentence that mistakenly uses general reference. The word or word group that refers back to its antecedents has been underlined for you.

Example ___*G*___ **1.** Heavy rain and high winds plagued the camping trip, <u>which</u> made us uncomfortable. [The word *which* seems to refer to many things: the rain, the winds, even the camping trip itself. In trying to refer to so much, the pronoun ends up referring to nothing specific or clear at all.]

_____ **1.** We carried tents, sleeping bags, clothes, and cooking gear, and <u>all this equipment</u> was a heavy load. [Does the word group *all this equipment* refer clearly to what is being carried?]

_____ **2.** The hills were steep, and the trail was muddy, <u>which</u> made our hike more difficult.

_____ **3.** Yesterday morning we packed our wet gear and covered ten miles of rough ground, but <u>that</u> didn't bother me.

GO ON

_____ **4.** When the clouds cleared, the stars and the moon shone brightly, <u>which</u> created a

pleasant and restful night.

_____ **5.** Challenges, surprises, and even setbacks—<u>these obstacles</u> have taught me a lot about

my own strength.

EXERCISE B Fix the unclear pronoun reference in each item below by rewriting each item on the line
provided. The unclear pronoun has been underlined for you.

Example 1. A marathon is longer than 26 miles, and <u>that</u> takes endurance. [The word *that* does

not clearly refer to any one thing, so *that* has been replaced by a specific reference,

running one.]

A marathon is longer than 26 miles, and running one takes endurance.

6. Myra's mother finished school and became a firefighter, <u>which</u> makes Myra proud.   [What
exactly makes Myra proud—her mother finishing school, her mother becoming a firefighter, or a
combination? You can decide, but replace *which* with a more specific word or words.]

_____

7. The volunteers raked leaves and put up a fence, and <u>it</u> was rewarding.

_____

8. Our neighbor has two cats and three birds, and <u>that</u> usually makes me sneeze.

_____

9. Waves splashed the dock, and a cold wind blew. <u>This</u> caused everyone to rush inside.

_____

10. The drive from Austin to Dallas took the family three hours, <u>which</u> was uneventful.

_____

Comparison of Modifiers

Degrees of Comparison

8d. Modifiers change form to show comparison.

The three forms of comparison are called *degrees of comparison.*

The *positive degree* consists of the base form of the modifier and is used when at least one thing is being described. The *comparative degree* usually consists of the base form of the modifier plus the ending *–er* or the word *more* and is used when two things are being compared. The *superlative degree* usually consists of the base form of the modifier plus the ending *–est* or the word *most* and is used when three or more things are being compared.

	POSITIVE	COMPARATIVE	SUPERLATIVE
ONE SYLLABLE	hot	hot**ter**	hot**test**
TWO SYLLABLES	jolly	jolli**er, more** jolly	jolli**est, most** jolly
THREE SYLLABLES	happily	**more** happily	**most** happily

All decreasing comparative degrees of comparison are formed by placing the word *less* in front of the modifier, and all decreasing superlative degrees of comparison are formed by placing the word *least* in front of the modifier.

	POSITIVE	COMPARATIVE	SUPERLATIVE
EXAMPLES	tall	**less** tall	**least** tall
	silly	**less** silly	**least** silly
	dangerous	**less** dangerous	**least** dangerous

EXERCISE A Fill in the blank in each of the following sentences with the correct form of the modifier suggested in parentheses at the end of the sentence.

Examples 1. Yesterday was _____sunnier_____ than today has been. (comparative degree of *sunny*)

[*Sunny* consists of two syllables, so *–er* can be used to form the comparative degree.]

2. Last year was the _____least rainy_____ year we've seen in over a decade. (decreasing superlative degree of *rainy*) [All decreasing superlative degrees use *least.*]

1. Is this movie _____ than that one? (comparative degree of *exciting*) [How many syllables are in *exciting*?]

2. That's the _____ handwriting of any president, ever! (superlative degree of *clear*)

3. Which one of the two lawns is _____? (comparative degree of *green*)

4. The test was _____ than I thought it would be. (comparative degree of *easy*)

GO ON

5. Of the five rubber bands, this one is _____. (decreasing superlative degree of *elastic*)

6. Which of these four bolts is _____ to fit? (superlative degree of *likely*)

7. This online encyclopedia is probably the _____ of all of those now available on the Internet. (superlative degree of *trustworthy*)

8. Reading the instructions would certainly be _____ than trying to figure out how to install brake shoes on our own. (comparative degree of *helpful*)

9. This time, find an exterior paint that is _____ than the original color. (decreasing comparative degree of *purple*)

10. There are _____ machine presses working today than there were yesterday. (comparative degree of *few*)

Use of Comparative and Superlative Forms

8e.   Use the comparative degree when comparing two things. Use the superlative degree when comparing more than two things.

> **EXAMPLES**   Shawna and Maria both raced, but Shawna ran **faster.** [The actions of two people are compared, *Shawna* and *Maria*, so *fast* is in the comparative degree.]
>
> Shawna, Maria, and Lucinda raced, but Shawna ran **fastest.** [The actions of more than two people are compared, *Shawna*, *Maria*, and *Lucinda*, so *fast* is in the superlative degree.]

EXERCISE B Decide whether the comparative degree or the superlative degree of the modifier is needed for each of the following sentences. Then, underline the correct form of the modifier.

Example 1. The story is (*more thrilling, most thrilling*) than the movie! [Only two items are being compared here, so the comparative degree of *thrilling* is needed.]

11. "A Sound of Thunder" is a scary story, but I think that "The Birds" has a (*scarier, scariest*) plot. [How many short stories are being compared in this sentence?]

12. Which bird species do you think is the (*most aggressive, more aggressive*) in the story, the gulls, the crows, or the jackdaws?

13. Our class thinks that Daphne du Maurier is a (*more challenging, most challenging*) writer to read than Ray Bradbury.

14. Is it (*harder, hardest*) to write a comedy, a mystery, or a horror story?

15. I think that scary stories are (*most difficult, more difficult*) to read than other kinds of stories.

Placement of Modifiers A

8i. Avoid using dangling modifiers.

Any modifying word, phrase, or clause that does not clearly or sensibly modify a word or word group in a sentence is a ***dangling modifier.*** A dangling modifier is not firmly attached to anything in the sentence, so it "dangles." When writers use dangling modifiers, they usually know what word they intended to modify but have forgotten to include that word in the sentence.

> **DANGLING** The wind turned from the north, shivering and reaching for an extra sweater. [The modifying phrase, *shivering and reaching for an extra sweater,* has nothing to modify in the sentence. The modified word is missing, so the modifier is dangling.]
>
> **CORRECT** The wind turned from the north; Todd found himself shivering and reaching for an extra sweater. [Now the modifying phrase, *shivering and reaching for an extra sweater,* clearly and sensibly modifies *Todd.*]

REMINDER Occasionally, a sentence uses *you* as its understood subject. A modifier describing *you* may look like it's dangling. Add the word *you* to the sentence to make sure that the modifier is not dangling.

> **EXAMPLE** When you are climbing the steepest hills, lean forward slightly.
> When you are climbing the steepest hills, **you** lean forward slightly. [It is now easy to see that the modifying clause *When you are climbing the steepest hills* clearly and sensibly modifies the understood subject *you.*]

EXERCISE A If the underlined modifier is dangling, write *D* for *dangling* on the line provided before each of the following sentences. If the underlined modifier clearly and sensibly modifies a word in the sentence, write *C* for *correct* on the blank provided.

Examples _____C_____ **1.** San Francisco, <u>lying on the coast of the Pacific</u>, is a hilly city. [The phrase *lying on the coast of the Pacific* clearly modifies *San Francisco,* so the modifier makes sense.]

_____D_____ **2.** <u>Situated on a fault</u>, earthquakes are a serious threat. [The phrase *Situated on a fault* is placed near *earthquakes,* but it does not modify *earthquakes* or any other word in the sentence. It is dangling.]

_____ **1.** <u>Riding in an air-conditioned car</u>, the hot sun was barely noticeable. [What word does the phrase *Riding in an air-conditioned car* modify? Does it make sense?]

_____ **2.** The TV picture flickered, <u>annoying the viewers</u>. [What word does the phrase *annoying the viewers* modify? Does it make sense?]

_____ **3.** <u>Peering under the edge of the sofa</u>, the library book was no longer missing.

_____ **4.** <u>Breathing slowly and clearing my mind</u>, relaxation was finally achieved. **GO ON**

_____ **5.** The fence, <u>built high and sturdily</u>, kept the dogs in the yard.

_____ **6.** <u>To edit the essay's spelling</u>, run the spell-checker and then read aloud.

_____ **7.** <u>Walking along the neatly edged sidewalk</u>, City Hall loomed ahead.

_____ **8.** The birdwatchers observed the cranes <u>migrating in formation</u>.

_____ **9.** <u>Named for his grandfather</u>, a sense of family history mattered greatly.

_____ **10.** <u>When alarmed</u>, the insects chatter noisily.

EXERCISE B Revise each of the following sentences so that the underlined dangling modifier will clearly and sensibly modify a word or word group in the revised sentence.

Example 1. <u>Sweating profusely</u>, weight lifting is a demanding sport.

> *Sweating profusely, Jacob discovered that weight lifting is a demanding sport.*

[The modifying phrase *Sweating profusely* now clearly and sensibly modifies *Jacob*.]

11. <u>Exhausted and thirsty</u>, the locker room looked welcoming. [What revision will make *exhausted and thirsty* clearly and sensibly modify a word or word group?]

_____

12. <u>Shimmering faintly</u>, we watched the first stars of the evening appear.

_____

13. <u>While disconnecting the car's battery</u>, the horn began to blow.

_____

14. <u>To successfully perform this experiment</u>, hours of preparation are needed.

_____

15. <u>Picking up the phone</u>, Tony's mom's voice was loud and clear.

_____

Placement of Modifiers B

8j.   Avoid using misplaced modifiers.

A word, phrase, or clause that seems to modify the wrong word or word group in a sentence is a *misplaced modifier*. Writers can avoid misplaced modifiers by taking care to place the modifier as close as possible to the word or word group being described.

> **MISPLACED**   Hanging in the museum, the art students stared in awe at the art. [The modifying phrase *Hanging in the museum* is closest to the word group *art students,* so it modifies *students* rather than *art.*]
>
> **CORRECT**   The art students stared in awe at the art hanging in the museum. [Now the modifying phrase is next to the word group it describes, and the sentence makes sense.]

EXERCISE A If the underlined modifier in each of the following sentences is misplaced, write *M* on the line provided. If the modifier modifies the correct word, write *C* for *correct.*

Example ___M___ **1.** Two lab assistants stood in the chemistry lab wearing white lab coats. [The phrase *wearing white lab coats* should modify *lab assistants,* but it follows the noun *lab.* It is misplaced.]

_____ **1.** Threatening to boil over, one assistant carefully watched a test tube. [Is the modifying phrase placed near the noun it modifies? Or is it misplaced?]

_____ **2.** Please get me a beaker with a lid on it from the cabinet.

_____ **3.** Changing colors, the assistants monitored the liquid in the beaker.

_____ **4.** Trying to make the experiment a success, every measurement was carefully noted by the assistants.

_____ **5.** Pleased with their work, the scientists praised the lab assistants.

> **TIP▶** Be especially careful to place adjective clauses beginning with words such as *that, which,* and *who* as near as possible to the words they modify.
>
> **MISPLACED**   Connect the mouse to the computer port that fits your hand most comfortably. [The clause *that fits your hand most comfortably* seems to describe *port.* The clause is misplaced.]
>
> **CORRECT**   Connect the mouse that fits your hand most comfortably to the computer port. [Now the modifying clause is close to the word it describes, *mouse,* and the sentence makes sense.]

GO ON▶

EXERCISE B Draw a line under the misplaced modifier in each of the following sentences.

Example 1. Do all of you have the assignment and a pencil or pen <u>that you need to finish</u>?

[Because the clause *that you need to finish* is intended to modify *assignment* rather than

pencil or pen, it is misplaced and should appear next to *assignment*.]

6. The painting covered the wall in its heavy gold frame. [Is there a prepositional phrase modifying

the wrong noun in this sentence?]

7. It's time to put the tools into the tool chest you were using to fix the car.

8. Rocking in her lap, Grandmother soothed her grandson.

9. Freshly picked from the tree, breakfast consisted of delicious peaches.

10. The flag was flapping in the wind, wrapping itself around the pole.

EXERCISE C Revise each of the following sentences so that the underlined misplaced modifier will
clearly and sensibly modify the correct word or group of words in the revised sentence.

Example 1. Flapping their wings loudly, the cats startled the sparrows into flight.

Flapping their wings loudly, the sparrows were startled into flight by the cats.

[*Flapping their wings loudly* now modifies the correct noun, *sparrows,* rather than *cats.*]

11. <u>Withered in the sun</u>, Janice regarded her garden with dismay. [Which noun is *Withered in the sun*

intended to modify?]

_____

12. Please bring me the book from the shelf <u>that has no back cover.</u>

_____

13. <u>Embedded in the rock</u>, the geologist tapped lightly on the crystals.

_____

14. The sun set as we watched <u>with a fiery glow.</u>

_____

15. The mouse skittered into the woodpile, <u>which wanted to hide from the hawk.</u>

_____

A Glossary of Usage A

a, an Use *a* before words that begin with a consonant sound. Use *an* before words that begin with a vowel sound. Keep in mind that the sound, not the actual letter, that a word begins with determines whether *a* or *an* should be used.

> **EXAMPLES** I found **a** beautiful seashell. [*Beautiful* begins with a consonant sound.]
>
> Is Colorado Avenue **a** one-way street? [*One* begins with a consonant sound, even though the written word begins with a vowel.]
>
> Ms. Martinez is **an** excellent coach. [*Excellent* begins with a vowel sound.]
>
> The drive takes about **an** hour. [*Hour* begins with a vowel sound, even though the written word begins with a consonant.]

accept, except *Accept* is a verb and means "to receive." *Except* can be used as a preposition meaning "excluding." *Except* also can be used as a verb meaning "to excuse," "to leave out," or "to omit."

> **EXAMPLES** The mayor **accepted** the committee's recommendations. [You can replace *accepted* with *received*.]
>
> All of the postcards are fifty cents **except** the oversized ones. [You can replace *except* with *excluding*.]
>
> Residents of the apartment complex are **excepted** from paying a rental fee for the community room. [You can replace *excepted* with *excused*.]

ain't *Ain't* is nonstandard English. Do not use *ain't* in formal writing and speaking.

> **NONSTANDARD** That bee **ain't** going to sting you.
> **STANDARD** That bee **isn't** going to sting you.

EXERCISE A Underline the word or word group in parentheses that is correct according to formal, standard English.

Examples 1. My grandmother painted all of those paintings *(except, accept)* the one in the

middle. [You can replace *except* with *excluding*.]

2. *(Isn't, Ain't)* the Pecan Festival this weekend? [*Ain't* is nonstandard.]

1. *(A, An)* owl once nested in our backyard. [Does the word *owl* start with a vowel sound or a

consonant sound?]

2. Will our honored guest *(except, accept)* this certificate of appreciation? [Which word can be

replaced with *receive*?]

3. *(I ain't, I'm not)* too sure about the answer to this math problem.

4. Every pencil needs to be sharpened *(except, accept)* this one.

5. Is this dresser *(a, an)* antique?

6. For our final project in science, my group created *(a, an)* Web site about black holes.

Developmental Language Skills

7. Carlos (*accepted, excepted*) the nomination for student-volunteer of the year.

8. Why (*ain't, aren't*) you going on the camping trip?

9. Have you ever seen (*an, a*) hourglass?

10. Nina was (*accepted, excepted*) from track practice for two weeks because she sprained her ankle.

---

a lot   *A lot* is two words, not one. Never write *a lot* as one word.

> **EXAMPLE**   We have **a lot** of yardwork to do today.

at   Do not use *at* after *where*.

> **NONSTANDARD**   **Where** did I leave my backpack **at?**
> **STANDARD**   **Where** did I leave my backpack?

among, between   Use *between* when you are referring to two individuals or items at a time. Use *among* when you are referring to a group.

> **EXAMPLES**   The lamp is **between** the desk and the bookcase. [*Between the desk and the bookcase* refers to two items, *desk* and *bookcase*.]
> You will find the file folder **among** the files in that cabinet. [*Among the files in that cabinet* refers to a group of items.]

EXERCISE B Underline the word or word group in parentheses that is correct according to formal, standard English.

Examples 1. Just (*between, among*) you and me, this milk tastes a little sour. [Two people are

referred to in the sentence, so *between* is correct.]

2. (*Alot, A lot*) of people attended the band concert last night. [*A lot* is two words.]

11. Where did John leave the library (*books, books at*)? [Should *at* be used after *where?*]

12. Divide the apple equally (*among, between*) the four children. [Is the sentence referring to individuals or a group?]

13. The squirrels gathered (*alot, a lot*) of pecans under the tree.

14. The CD fell (*between, among*) the desk and wall, and I can't reach it.

15. I'm glad that I proofread my paper; I had made (*alot, a lot*) of typos.

16. Can you tell me where the canned vegetables (*are, are at*)?

17. The final soccer game was (*among, between*) the Cougars and the Hurricanes.

18. Your baby brother sleeps (*alot, a lot*)!

19. Is that your dog sitting (*among, between*) the five garden gnomes?

20. Where will the car wash (*be, be at*)?

A Glossary of Usage B

bring, take   *Bring* means "to come carrying something." *Take* means "to go carrying something." Think of *bring* as related to *come,* and *take* as related to *go.*

> **EXAMPLES**   Please **bring** me the stapler when you come to my desk.
>
> Will you **take** these worksheets when you go to the copy room?

could of   Do not write *of* with the helping verb *could.* Write *could have.* Also use *have* after *ought to, should, would, might,* and *must.* When you speak, you may often pronounce the helping verb *have* as *of,* especially with the contraction *could've.* However, you should only write it as *have.*

> **EXAMPLES**   Stan **could have/could've** [not *could of*] told us he was here.
>
> He **might have/might've** [not *might of*] let us know!

fewer, less   Use *fewer* with plural nouns. Use *less* with singular nouns. *Fewer* tells "how many"; *less* tells "how much."

> **EXAMPLES**   **Fewer** students enrolled in summer school this year. [*Students* is plural, so *fewer* is used.]
>
> **Less** salt is needed than you might think. [*Salt* is singular, so *less* is used.]

EXERCISE A   Underline the word or word group in parentheses that is correct according to formal, standard English.

Examples 1. We *(might of, might have)* lost the game without your help! [The helping verb *have* should be used with *might.*]

   2. *(Take, Bring)* your bathing suit when you come visit us at the beach. [*Bring* means "to come carrying something."]

1. Dave scored *(less, fewer)* points than Marco did in the last game. [Is *points* singular or plural?]

2. Would you please *(take, bring)* the casserole when you go to the potluck dinner? [Which word means "to go carrying something"?]

3. The parrot *(must have, must of)* taught itself to imitate the sound of a ringing phone.

4. When you come back from the store, please *(take, bring)* in the mail.

5. Try to think positive and spend *(less, fewer)* time worrying.

6. *(Bring, Take)* this book to your aunt the next time you go for a visit.

7. Our new car uses *(less, fewer)* gasoline than our old one did.

8. The computer *(should have, should of)* arrived today.

9. Does your brother drink *(less, fewer)* soft drinks than he used to?

10. The electricity *(must of, must have)* gone out last night.

good, well   *Good* is an adjective. Do not use *good* to modify a verb; use *well*, which can be used as an adverb.

>   **EXAMPLES**   She made a **good** impression on stage. [*Good* is an adjective that tells what kind of impression.]
>   Did Jessie perform **well** at the recital? [*Well* is an adverb that tells how Jessie performed.]

hisself, theirself, theirselves   Avoid using these nonstandard words in formal writing and speaking. Use *himself* and *themselves*.

>   **EXAMPLES**   Kyle congratulated **himself** [not *hisself*] on a job well done.
>   The decorating committee really outdid **themselves** [not *theirselves*]!

it's, its   *Its* means "belonging to it." *It's* is a contraction of *it is* or *it has*.

>   **EXAMPLES**   The bird was startled by **its** reflection in the mirror. [*Its* in this sentence means "belonging to the bird."]
>   **It's** an honor to be elected president of the student council. [*It's* is a contraction of *it is*.]
>   **It's** been a wonderful day. [*It's* is a contraction of *It has*.]

kind of, sort of   In formal writing and speaking, avoid using *kind of* and *sort of*. Use *somewhat* or *rather*.

>   **INFORMAL**   I'm kind of nervous about giving a speech.
>   **FORMAL**   I'm **rather** nervous about giving a speech.

EXERCISE B Underline the word or word group in parentheses that is correct according to formal, standard English.

Examples 1. (*It's*, *Its*) about time you arrived! [*It's* is a contraction of *It is*.]

2. Did you do (*good*, *well*) on the quiz? [The adverb *well* modifies the verb phrase *Did do*.]

11. My dog likes to have (*its*, *it's*) tummy rubbed. [Which word shows possession?]

12. Your dad cooks really (*well*, *good*). [Which word should modify the verb *cooks*?]

13. All of the team members challenge (*theirselves*, *themselves*) to meet weekly goals.

14. The judges were (*kind of*, *rather*) impressed by the quality of the students' artwork.

15. (*Its*, *It's*) been three years since our last trip to the Grand Canyon.

16. Josh asked (*himself*, *hisself*), "How can I do better next time?"

17. How quietly the hummingbird beats (*its*, *it's*) wings!

18. It was (*kind or*, *rather*) hot yesterday afternoon.

19. Getting a (*good*, *well*) night's sleep is very important.

20. (*Its*, *It's*) time for the concert to begin.

A Glossary of Usage C

than, then   *Than* is a word used in making comparisons. *Then* means "next" or "at that time."

> **EXAMPLES** It was colder today **than** it was yesterday. [*Than* is used to make a comparison between the temperature today and yesterday.]
>
> Megan will research the subject, and **then** she will write the report. [*Then* indicates what Megan will do "next."]

their, there, they're   *Their* is the possessive form of *they* and means "belonging to them." *There* is used to mean "at that place" or to begin a sentence. *They're* is a contraction of *they are.*

> **EXAMPLES** The twins went to visit **their** aunt. [*Their* in this sentence means "belonging to the twins."]
>
> Put the silverware over **there.** [*There* means "at that place."]
>
> **There** are thousands of wildflowers in that field! [*There* begins the sentence.]
>
> **They're** ready for the camping trip. [*They're* is a contraction of *They are.*]

them   *Them* should not be used as an adjective in formal writing and speaking. Use *those.*

> **EXAMPLE** **Those** [not *them*] apples are as ripe as they can be.

EXERCISE A Underline the word or word group in parentheses that is correct according to formal, standard English.

Example 1. Who can run faster *(then, <u>than</u>)* I can? [*Than* is used to make comparisons.]

1. *(Their, They're, There)* are over fifty volunteer opportunities listed in today's paper! [Which word is used to begin a sentence?]

2. *(Them, Those)* books are heavy.

3. How many students are willing to volunteer *(there, their, they're)* time?

4. The detective opened the door just a crack and *(than, then)* peered inside.

5. The dogs wagged *(their, they're, there)* tails.

try and   In formal writing and speaking, use *try to,* not *try and.*

> **EXAMPLE** **Try to** [not *try and*] reach that pear, since you're taller than I am.

your, you're   *Your* is a possessive form of *you.* It means "belonging to you." *You're* is the contraction of *you are.*

> **EXAMPLES** Is that **your** report lying on the desk? [*Your* shows possession.]
>
> **You're** not afraid of insects, are you? [*You're* is the contraction of *You are.*]

EXERCISE B Underline the word or word group in parentheses that is correct according to formal, standard English.

Example 1. (<u>Try to</u>, *Try and*) make it to the finish line! [*Try to* is formal, standard English.]

6. How many different types of vegetables do you have in *(you're, your)* garden? [Which word means "belonging to you"?]

7. The drama club will *(try to, try and)* make their own costumes for the play.

8. Congratulations! *(You're, Your)* the winner of the essay contest.

9. When is *(you're, your)* soccer game?

10. Does your cat *(try and, try to)* tear open the bag of cat food, too?

Double Negatives

hardly, scarcely   Do not use *hardly* or *scarcely* with another negative word in formal writing and speaking.

> **EXAMPLES**   That bird **is** [not *isn't*] **hardly** gaining any distance because it's flying against the wind.
>
> The conference room **has** [not *hasn't*] **scarcely** enough chairs for everyone.

no, nothing, none   Do not use *no, nothing,* or *none* with another negative word in formal writing and speaking.

> **NONSTANDARD**   We don't need no help with this project.
> **STANDARD**   We need **no** help with this project.
> **STANDARD**   We **don't** need any help with this project.
>
> **NONSTANDARD**   I wanted to buy a book about aquariums, but I couldn't find none.
> **STANDARD**   I wanted to buy a book about aquariums, but I **couldn't** find **one.**

EXERCISE C Underline the word or word group in parentheses that is correct according to formal, standard English.

Example 1. Please, don't add (*no*, <u>any</u>) sugar to my cereal. [*Don't* is a negative word, so the word *any* should be used.]

11. The class doesn't have *(no, any)* prerequisites. [Which word should be used with the negative word *doesn't?*]

12. Once I put on Boxer's leash, he *(can, cannot)* hardly wait to get outside and go for a walk.

13. I haven't got *(nothing, anything)* to lose by applying for the scholarship.

14. *(Have, Haven't)* none of the cocoons opened yet?

15. Nobody has *(any, no)* idea how long the game will last.

Capitalization A

First Words

10a.	Capitalize the first word in every sentence.

> **EXAMPLE**   **T**he trees are shedding their leaves. [*The* is the first word of the sentence.]

10c.	Capitalize the first word of a directly quoted sentence, even when the quoted sentence appears in the middle of a longer sentence.

> **EXAMPLES**   My friend Amy said, "**Y**ou can borrow my sister's bicycle." [*You* is capitalized because it is the first word of the sentence quoted within a longer sentence.]
>
> "**H**er bike helmet is in the closet," mentioned Amy. [*Her* is capitalized because it is the first word of the sentence that is quoted. *Her* is also the first word of the longer sentence.]

EXERCISE A Circle the letter that should be capitalized in each of the following sentences.

Examples 1. m̲y desk has been moved into another row. [The *m* in *my* should be capitalized because it is the first word of the sentence.]

2. Suddenly, the tour guide announced, "l̲ook, everyone, there is a red fox behind that tree." [The *l* in *look* should be capitalized because it is the first word in a quoted sentence.]

1. I think she said, "please take your shoes out of the kitchen." [Is the first word of the quoted sentence capitalized?]

2. "who has my pencil?" asked Maria. [Is the first word of the sentence capitalized?]

3. Daniel smiled and said, "boy, this movie's ending sure surprised me."

4. some of the most well-known features of that national park are its glaciers.

5. Her eyes grew wide and she whispered, "did you hear that?"

6. he says that he's going to try out for our soccer team this year.

7. it'll be wonderful to add a trophy or two to the cases in the front hallway.

8. My father nodded and said, "the metal frame of this dock was made to last."

9. as long as we're standing here, keep your chin up and your shoulders back.

10. how many blades are on the propeller of that helicopter?

GO ON

Letter Salutations and Closings

10d. Capitalize the first word in both the salutation and the closing of a letter.

The salutation is the part of the letter in which you greet the person to whom you are writing. The closing is the part of the letter immediately before your signature.

> **SALUTATIONS** **D**ear Dr. Monroe: **M**y dearest Raul,
>
> **CLOSINGS** **S**incerely,   **W**ishing you the best,

NOTE▶ Except for names and titles, the first word is the only word that is capitalized in a salutation or closing. In the previous examples, the abbreviation *Dr.* is capitalized because it is a title, and *Monroe* is capitalized because it is a person's name.

EXERCISE B Circle the letter that should be capitalized in each salutation or closing.

Example 1. Ⓦith deepest gratitude, [The *w* in *with* should be capitalized because it is the first letter of the closing of a letter.]

11. my dearest Miss Bennet, [Is the first letter of the salutation capitalized?]

12. yours faithfully,

13. dear Service Manager:

14. sincerely yours,

15. dear Mom and Dad,

The Pronoun *I*

10e. The pronoun *I* is always capitalized.

> **EXAMPLES** Which one of these jackets should **I** wear today?
>
> If you wash the dishes, **I'll** dry them. [The pronoun *I* is always capitalized, even when it appears in the contraction of *I will*.]

EXERCISE C Circle the letter that should be capitalized in each of the following sentences.

Example 1. Sheila announced, "Trimming my own bangs was easier than Ⓘ thought it would be." [The pronoun *I* should always be capitalized.]

16. In every one of my photographs, i look sleepy. [Is the pronoun *I* capitalized?]

17. "We are going to pick up the package," i told them.

18. Maybe i'm in the mood for a long stroll.

19. "Perhaps," Chi laughed, "he and i should rewrite the letter."

20. You would think that i'd never eaten spaghetti before.

Capitalization B

10f. Capitalize proper nouns.

A *proper noun* names a particular person, place, thing, or idea. Proper nouns are capitalized. A *common noun* names a kind or type of person, place, thing, or idea. A common noun generally is not capitalized unless it begins a sentence or is part of a title.

PROPER NOUNS	Nelson Mandela	Yosemite Falls	Comets	Stoicism
COMMON NOUNS	leader	waterfall	team	philosophy

TIP To find a proper noun in a sentence, try this test. Look for the nouns in the sentence. Then, look at each noun by itself, covering up the rest of the sentence. Do you still know exactly who or what is meant? If so, the noun is probably a proper noun.

EXAMPLE My uncle met Aunt Kara while they were still in high school. [If you were to look at the noun *uncle* by itself, you would be left wondering which uncle is meant. *Uncle* is a common noun. On the other hand, if you were to look at the noun *Aunt Kara* by itself, you would still know exactly who is meant. *Aunt Kara* is a proper noun.]

EXERCISE A Circle the word or word group in each pair that is capitalized correctly.

Examples 1. a. Thomas stearns Eliot   **b.** (James Madison) [The name *James Madison* is correctly capitalized. The *s* in *Stearns* should have been capitalized.]

2. a. (Thomas More)   **b.** Historical figure [The name *Thomas More* is correctly capitalized. *Historical* should not have been capitalized, because *historical figure* is not a specific person.]

1. a. two Streets away   **b.** Madison Avenue

[Which word or word group is a correctly capitalized proper noun?]

2. a. july   **b.** month

[Which word is not a proper noun and is correct without a capital letter?]

3. a. Fisk elementary school   **b.** Carver Middle School

4. a. Wednesday   **b.** Weekday

5. a. San Antonio Spurs   **b.** Basketball team

6. a. a famous King   **b.** Queen Victoria

7. a. hero   **b.** frances mostern

8. a. west Virginia   **b.** Idaho

9. a. those limestone caves   **b.** Carlsbad Caverns national park

10. a. Boston   **b.** City

GO ON

People, Animals, and Initials

Capitalize the names and initials of people and the names of animals.

PEOPLE	Eleanora Holiday	Francis Scott Key	E. B. White
	Catherine of Braganza	William the Conqueror	Charles the Fair
ANIMALS	Shamoo	Laddie	Rover

NOTE Some proper nouns consist of more than one word. In these names, prepositions of fewer than five letters (*at, in, of, on, over,* and so on) and articles (*a, an,* and *the*) are generally not capitalized.

EXAMPLES Billy the Kid [*The* is not capitalized because it is an article.]

Gulf of Mexico [*Of* is not capitalized because it is a short preposition.]

EXERCISE B Fill in each blank with a proper noun that corresponds to the underlined common noun in each of the following sentences. Be sure to capitalize correctly the proper nouns that you write. Hint: You can make up a name if you don't know of one.

Examples 1. _____Richard Wright_____ is one of my favorite authors. [*Richard Wright* is a proper noun because it is the name of a specific writer.]

2. Gabrielle is visiting her favorite relative, _____Aunt Mary_____. [*Aunt Mary* is a proper noun because it names a specific relative of Gabrielle's.]

11. The funniest person I have ever met is named _____. [Have you filled in the blank with the name of someone funny and capitalized it correctly?]

12. She named her horse _____. [Have you filled in the blank with the name of a horse and capitalized it correctly?]

13. The coach says that his middle name is _____.

14. Her favorite author is _____.

15. Her neighbor, _____, likes to jog in the morning.

16. My best friend's first name, middle initial, and last name are _____.

17. She decided to name her pet dog _____.

18. When he sang, he sounded like the famous singer _____.

19. One afternoon, she met the popular actress _____.

20. The first U.S. president that comes to mind is _____.

for **CHAPTER 10: CAPITAL LETTERS**   *pages 295–298*

Capitalization C
Geographical Names

Capitalize geographical names, including the names of towns and cities, counties, townships, provinces, states, countries, continents, islands, mountains, bodies of water, parks and forests, regions, roads, streets, highways, and other geographical names.

EXAMPLES	**B**astrop [town]	**P**atna [city]
	Hennepin **C**ounty [county]	**M**issouri [state]
	Mexico [country]	**A**sia [continent]
	Osumi **I**slands [islands]	**M**ount **R**ainier [mountain]
	Loch **N**ess [body of water]	**B**ig **B**end **N**ational **P**ark [park]
	Fishlake **N**ational **F**orest [forest]	**P**ennsylvania **T**urnpike [highway]
	County **R**oad 884 [road]	**P**ark **S**treet [street]

NOTE Some geographical names consist of more than one word. In these names, prepositions of fewer than five letters (*at, in, of, on, over,* and so on) and articles (*a, an,* and *the*) are generally not capitalized.

      EXAMPLES   Bay **of** Bengal [The short preposition *of* is not capitalized.]
                         Tomb **of t**he Unknown Soldier [The short preposition *of* is not capitalized. The article *the* is not capitalized.]

EXERCISE A In each sentence below, circle the letter that should be capitalized.

Examples 1. He is from a little town called Ⓚerrville. [The *k* in *kerrville* should be capitalized because it names a specific town.]

      2. My favorite recreational spot is near Delaware Ⓑay. [The *b* in *bay* should be capitalized because it is part of a name of a specific body of water.]

1. My closest relatives live in pasadena. [Is the name of a city capitalized?]

2. One of his cousins went snorkeling near the Great Barrier reef. [Is each word that is part of the name of a particular geographical feature capitalized?]

3. Any animal that can survive the weather in antarctica deserves to be studied.

4. We should visit grasslands National Park someday.

5. Peru is a country located in south America.

6. This book contains a picture of the rock of Gibraltar.

7. Each fall, our town holds a festival on lucinda Avenue.

8. We can only marvel at the length of the Colorado river.

9. She dreams of living close to the beaches in hawaii.

10. The band marched up Fourth street, and then it headed down Fifth.

Organizations, Teams, Institutions, and Government Bodies

Capitalize the names of organizations, teams, institutions, and government bodies.

> **EXAMPLES**   **F**isk **B**and **B**oosters [organization]   **W**ildcats [team]
>
> **S**upreme **C**ourt [government body]   **U**niversity of **C**hicago [institution]

> **NOTE▶** The names of some organizations and institutions consist of more than one word. In these names, prepositions of fewer than five letters (*at, in, of, on, over,* and so on) and articles (*a, an,* and *the*) are generally not capitalized.
>
> **EXAMPLE**   **U**niversity **of** **M**ichigan [*Of* is not capitalized because it is a short preposition.]

EXERCISE B Circle the word group that is capitalized correctly in each of the following pairs.

Example 1. a. Boston college   **b.** (House of Representatives) [Names of institutions and government bodies should be capitalized, so *House of Representatives* is the word group that is capitalized correctly.]

11. a. Eastvale Falcons   **b.** Bridgetown bulldogs

[Should names of teams be capitalized?]

12. a. Haywood city council   **b.** New York Court of Appeals

13. a. Smithsonian institution   **b.** Metropolitan Museum of Art

14. a. United States Senate   **b.** House of commons

15. a. Plano community college   **b.** University of Southern California

EXERCISE C Circle the letter or letters that should be capitalized in each of the following sentences. Hint: Geographical names, government bodies, teams, organizations, and institutions should be capitalized.

Example 1. A federal prison was once in use on a small island in ⓈanⒻrancisco Ⓑay. [*San Francisco Bay* should be capitalized because it is the name of a body of water.]

16. Making laws in the United States is complicated, and the governmental body called the house of representatives is a big part of that process. [Have you capitalized each word that is part of the name of a particular governmental body?]

17. The krishna river is a river that flows in the southern part of india.

18. Did Aunt Jessie see many different kinds of birds as she drove through Klamath national Forest in california?

19. When she gets older, Myra wants to play basketball for the university of texas longhorns.

20. Have you seen a picture of the sydney opera house, that famous building in australia?

Capitalization D

Special Events, Holidays, Calendar Items, and Historical Events and Periods

Capitalize the names of special events, holidays, calendar items, and historical events and periods.

| **EXAMPLES** | **B**oston **M**arathon | **N**ew **Y**ear's **D**ay | **J**une |
| | **A**merican **R**evolution | **H**omeric period | **M**onday |

NOTE The names of the seasons usually are not capitalized. Capitalize a season only if it is being personified or used in the name of a special event.

EXAMPLES Last **s**pring, Tina and Mrs. Diaz repainted the front deck. [*Spring* is not capitalized because it is not being personified or used in the name of a special event.]

One line of the poem reads, "O **S**pring, bring us your rains, your lilacs, your warmth!" [*Spring* is capitalized because it is being personified, or being treated as though it has human qualities.]

What was your favorite booth at the Valleytown **S**pring Carnival? [*Spring* is capitalized because it is used in the name of a special event.]

EXERCISE A Circle the letter or letters that should be capitalized in each of the following sentences.

Examples 1. The d̲ark Ages were not so unenlightened as we may imagine. [The *d* in *dark* should be capitalized because it is part of a name of a specific historical period.]

2. The day of Yom k̲ippur is a Jewish day of prayer and meditation. [The *k* in *kippur* should be capitalized because it is part of a name of a specific holy day.]

1. The day we now call presidents' Day used to be called Washington's Birthday. [Does the sentence contain the name of a holiday that needs to be capitalized?]

2. The scientists discovered a dinosaur bone from the jurassic era. [Does the sentence contain the name of a historical period that needs to be capitalized?]

3. Will we have a picnic to celebrate the fourth of July?

4. The season of spring begins in march.

5. At the end of January, Lee's family always celebrates the festival called tet.

6. During the parade on Arbor day, he rode on a float shaped like a tree.

7. She dreams that she will one day be able to play in the World series.

8. I think our trip should be on a saturday.

9. Sheila said that today was the holiday purim.

10. Many forms of art began to flourish during the renaissance.

Developmental Language Skills

Nationalities, Races, and Peoples

Capitalize the names of nationalities, races, and peoples.

EXAMPLES a **H**opi   a **G**eorgian   a **S**outh **A**frican
            the **B**ritish   the **D**utch   the **L**ebanese

EXERCISE B Circle the word or word group in each of the following pairs that is capitalized correctly.

Example 1. a. a brazilian   **b.** (an Australian) [The nationality *Australian* is capitalized correctly.]

11. a. italians   **b.** African Americans

   [Which name of a group of people is capitalized correctly?]

12. a. an Asian   **b.** a zuni

13. a. the romans   **b.** the Greeks

14. a. a caucasian   **b.** a Bantu

15. a. American Indians   **b.** hispanics

Businesses and Brand Names; Ships, Trains, Aircraft, and Spacecraft

Capitalize the names of ships, trains, aircraft, and spacecraft as well as the names of businesses and the brand names of business products.

EXAMPLES *Calypso* [name of a ship]   *Orient Express* [name of a train]
            Air Force One [name of an aircraft]   *Eagle* [name of a spacecraft]
            Sue's **D**esigns [name of a business] **E**conorent [brand name]
            Kleenex [name of a business product]

EXERCISE C Fill in each blank with a proper noun that corresponds to the underlined common noun in each of the following sentences. Be sure to capitalize correctly the proper nouns that you write. Hint: You can make up a name if you don't know of one.

Example 1. They took a <u>ship</u> called the ___*Queen Mary*___ across the Atlantic. [*Queen Mary* is a

   proper noun because it is the name of a specific ship.]

16. My aunt flies a small <u>plane</u> she named _____. [Have you written the name of a

   specific plane and capitalized it correctly?]

17. Her mother works for _____, a <u>business</u> that designs greeting cards.

18. We took a <u>train</u> ride aboard _____, an old steam-driven locomotive.

19. The <u>space shuttle</u> _____ has docked with the International Space Station.

20. I usually write with a _____, my favorite <u>brand</u> of pen.

Capitalization E

Buildings, Monuments, Memorials, and Awards

Capitalize the names of buildings and other structures, monuments, memorials, and awards.

EXAMPLES Empire State Building   Lincoln Memorial
Caldecott Medal   Academy Award

NOTE▶ Except when used as the first word in a sentence, the word *the* is not usually capitalized, even if it is part of a name. In *the Newbery Medal,* for example, *Newbery Medal* is capitalized while the word *the* is not.

EXERCISE A Circle the letter or letters that should be capitalized in each of the following sentences.

Example 1. For her discovery of radium, Marie Curie won a Nobel ⓟrize. [The *p* in *prize* should be capitalized because it is the name of an award.]

1. When Clara toured San Francisco, she took pictures of the golden gate bridge. [Does the sentence contain the name of a structure, and is that name capitalized?]

2. Someday, the pulitzer Prize is going to go to my next-door neighbor.

3. He really deserves an oscar for his performance after school.

4. Our teacher said that he wanted to stand at the base of the empire state building and look straight upward.

5. Alex and Justin counted all of the steps leading to the top of the statue of liberty.

Religious Names

Capitalize the names of religions and their followers, holy days and celebrations, sacred writings, and specific deities.

EXAMPLES Catholicism [religion]   Puritans [religious followers]
Passover [holy days]   Ashura [religious celebration]
Torah [sacred writings]   Allah [deity]

EXERCISE B Circle the letter that should be capitalized in each of the following sentences.

Example 1. That college class will study the prayers found in the sacred writings called the ⓥedas. [The *v* in *vedas* should be capitalized because *Vedas* is the name of a sacred writing.]

6. The hero of the story was lost at sea because he angered the god poseidon. [Is there the name of a specific deity that needs to be capitalized in the sentence?]

7. What is the name of the first book of the bible?

GO ON ▶

Developmental Language Skills   **113**

8. Because his family observes the holy days of ramadan, he and his brother are fasting from

dawn to sunset.

9. As the famous buddhist began to explain his spiritual beliefs, the audience grew quiet.

10. Christians everywhere will celebrate easter very soon.

Planets, Stars, and Constellations

10f. Capitalize the names of specific planets, stars, constellations, and other heavenly bodies.

> **EXAMPLES** **Me**rcury [planet]   **R**igel [star]
> **U**rsa **M**inor [constellation]   the **M**ilky **W**ay [galaxy]

NOTE The words *earth, sun,* and *moon* are generally not capitalized unless they are used as
specific bodies in the solar system.

> **EXAMPLES** The planet **E**arth is the third planet. [*Earth* is capitalized because it refers to
> part of the solar system.]
> We all live on the **e**arth. [In this sentence, *earth* is not capitalized.]

EXERCISE C Fill in the blanks with proper nouns that correspond to each of the common nouns that are
underlined in the sentences below. Be sure to capitalize correctly the proper nouns that you write. Hint:
You can make up any names if you don't know of one.

Example 1. The planet _____*Mars*_____ was once thought to be inhabited. [*Mars* is a proper

noun and should be capitalized because it is the name of a specific planet.]

11. On a clear, light-free night, the galaxy _____ is visible. [Have you filled in the

blank with the name of a galaxy and capitalized it correctly?]

12. Mike thought he saw a UFO, but it was really just the planet _____.

13. My favorite constellation is _____ because it is so easy to spot.

14. That comet, called _____, is an immense pool of interstellar gas.

15. The small-looking star _____ guided explorers as they traveled.

Capitalization F
School Subjects

Capitalize the names of language classes or course names that contain a number.

>   **EXAMPLES**   our **G**erman class   **T**rigonometry I
>   **M**athematics 1301   **g**eometry

EXERCISE A   Circle the word or word group that is capitalized correctly in each of the following pairs.

Example 1. a. (French)   **b.** World Literature   [*French* is the name of a language class and should

>   be capitalized.]

1. a. algebra I   **b.** Civics 101

[Should course names with numbers be capitalized?]

2. a. Geology 3300   **b.** American History

3. a. journalism II   **b.** Creative Writing 2

4. a. English   **b.** german

5. a. Physics 1   **b.** Astronomy

NOTE When capitalizing school subjects, do not capitalize short prepositions (*at, in, of, on, over,* and so on), articles (*a, an,* and *the*), coordinating conjunctions (*and, but,* and *or*), or the word *to* in infinitive verb forms unless they begin the name.

>   **EXAMPLES**   History **of** Civilization II [In the school subject *History of Civilization II,* the word *of* is not capitalized because it is a short preposition.]
>   Living **to** Learn 101 [In the school subject *Living to Learn 101,* the word *to* is not capitalized because it is part of the infinitive verb form *to learn.*]

EXERCISE B   Put a slash mark through each capital letter that should be lowercased, and circle each lowercase letter that should be capitalized in the following sentences.

Example 1. Didn't your mom take a class called Gardening /In /The ©ity 2? [The word *in* is a short

>   preposition, so it should be lowercased. *The* is an article, so it should be lowercased. *City*

>   is a noun, so it should be capitalized.]

6. Some high school students will take Chemistry. [Should general subjects be capitalized?]

7. Next Saturday there will be a class for mountain bikers, Bicycle maintenance I, at the school.

8. I wonder what will be taught in the community class called Conversational japanese III.

GO ON ▶

9. Will Jamal be taking journalism 101 during his first year of high school?

10. Mrs. Tanaka will be teaching the summer-camp class called spanish I.

Proper Adjectives

10f. Capitalize proper adjectives.

Proper adjectives are adjectives that are formed from proper nouns. Since proper nouns are capitalized, proper adjectives are capitalized, too. In many cases, proper adjectives are formed by giving the proper noun a different ending, such as *–ish, –ese, –ic, –ian,* or *–an.* Some proper adjectives are exactly the same form as the proper noun.

> **EXAMPLES** **I**rish [formed from the proper noun *Ireland*]
> **C**hinese [formed from the proper noun *China*]
> **P**latonic [formed from the proper noun *Plato*]
> **B**ostonian [formed from the proper noun *Boston*]
> **S**hakespearean [formed from the proper noun *Shakespeare*]
> **C**herokee [has same form as the proper noun *Cherokee*]

EXERCISE C Circle the letter that should be capitalized in each of the following sentences.

Examples 1. We used to live in an old (V)ictorian mansion. [The word *Victorian* is a proper adjective created from the proper noun *Victoria,* so it should be capitalized.]

2. The teacher explained (A)ristotelian thinking, which is named for a famous philosopher. [The word *Aristotelian* is a proper adjective created from the proper noun *Aristotle,* so it should be capitalized.]

11. The alaskan landscape is home to bears, whales, and moose. [Is there a proper adjective that has been created from the name of a specific state? Has that adjective been capitalized?]

12. Tessa is studying roman architecture at the local community college. [Is there a proper adjective that has been created from the name of a specific place? Has that adjective been capitalized?]

13. A scottish bagpipe player is on the cover of that book about music in Scotland.

14. Because the Arctic is such a cold place, I have always admired the endurance of arctic animals.

15. Our neighbors, who want to visit Portugal one day, collect portuguese sculpture.

16. Have you noticed that this restaurant has a hollywood theme?

17. Her hockey team's only canadian player is an especially fast skater.

18. Using the japanese tea garden as a backdrop, the photographer snapped many shots.

19. Rosa wears the most beautiful spanish dresses.

20. Prepare yourself for another minnesotan winter.

Capitalization G

Titles of Persons

Capitalize professional, military, civil, official, and noble titles of persons when the title appears immediately before the person's name.

> **EXAMPLES**   **D**octor Wasser [professional title]   **C**aptain Martinez [military title]
>
> **M**ayor Smith [civil title]   **R**epresentative Tupa [official title]
>
> **K**ing George [noble title]

> **NOTE**▶ When a title is used alone or following a person's name, the title usually is not capitalized, especially when *a* or *the* comes before the title.

> **EXAMPLES**   The **p**resident who was our history teacher's favorite was Thomas Jefferson. [Since the word *The* comes before the word *president*, *president* is not capitalized.]
>
> Thomas Jefferson, an interesting person and **p**resident, was our history teacher's favorite. [*President* comes after the name *Thomas Jefferson*, so *president* is not capitalized.]

EXERCISE A   Circle the letter that should be capitalized in each of the following sentences.

Examples 1. We watched ⓟrince William shake the minister's hand. [*Prince* should be capitalized because it is a title that comes before a person's name.]

2. My cast is actually the handiwork of ⓓoctor Margolis. [*Doctor* should be capitalized because it is a title that comes before a person's name.]

1. The man who teaches my weekend computer class is named professor Cho. [Does this sentence contain a professional title that comes before a person's name?]

2. I am reading an interesting article on the life of emperor Augustus. [Does this sentence contain a title of nobility that comes before a person's name?]

3. He probably never dreamed that one day he would be known as sir Paul McCartney.

4. My favorite justice has always been justice Potter Stewart.

5. One of our country's least popular presidents may have been president Millard Fillmore.

6. She spoke with deacon Callison about the grand opening of the new park.

7. According to senator Hawley, getting elected is far more difficult than serving in office.

8. Using cowpox germs, sir Edward Jenner developed a vaccination for smallpox.

9. The first professional woman astronomer in the United States was professor Maria Mitchell.

10. Our class met briefly with rabbi Goldmann.

GO ON ➡

Titles of Creative Works

Capitalize the titles of creative works, including books, articles, songs, poems, movies, television programs, musical compositions, paintings, sculptures, and plays.

EXAMPLES *The Joy Luck Club* [book]   "How to Fly a Kite" [article]
"America the Beautiful" [song]   "The Red Wheelbarrow" [poem]
Casablanca [movie]   *Biography* [television series]
The Four Seasons [musical composition]   *Starry Night* [painting]

EXERCISE B Circle the title that is capitalized correctly in each pair. In case you are unfamiliar with any of the titles, each title is followed by a bracketed description of the type of work.

Example 1. a. (Swan Lake) [musical composition]   **b.** *A midsummer night's dream* [play]

[*Swan Lake* is correctly capitalized. Each word in *A Midsummer Night's Dream* should be

capitalized.]

11. a. "Loveliest Of Trees" [poem]   **b.** "What Is Enlightenment?" [article]

[Which word should be lowercased because it is considered unimportant—*of* or *is*?]

12. a. "This Land is Your Land" [song]   **b.** "Finding the Right Sunscreen" [article]

13. a. "Mother to Son" [poem]   **b.** "Battle Hymn Of The Republic" [song]

14. a. *A Tale Of Two Cities* [book]   **b.** *Mona Lisa* [painting]

15. a. *I Never Sang For My Father* [play]   **b.** *Rhapsody in Blue* [musical composition]

EXERCISE C Circle any letters that should be capitalized in the following sentences. Put a slash (/) through any letters that are capitalized but should not be.

Example 1. Was Shakespeare thinking of a certain person when he wrote the poem "Shall I

Compare Thee /To a Summer's (d)ay?" [*To* should be lowercased because it is a short

preposition. *Day* should be capitalized because it is an important noun.]

16. Carrie's copy of the book *A Walk In the woods* has a photo of a bear on the cover. [Which

unimportant word has been incorrectly capitalized? Which important word needs to be capitalized?]

17. What is the topic of that article, "Bravery in an unexpected Place," that Ruben is reading?

18. The bright blues, reds, and yellows in the collage *Harriet Tubman And The Freedom Train* make

this lively piece of artwork noticeable.

19. The movie *Father Of the bride* made my dad laugh.

20. The Miles Davis CD called *Kind Of Blue* has jazz performances that include saxophone, piano,

bass, and drums.

End Marks and Abbreviations

End Marks

11a. A statement (or declarative sentence) is followed by a period.

> **EXAMPLE** Samuel plays the trombone. [The sentence is a statement, so it is followed by a period.]

11b. A question (or interrogative sentence) is followed by a question mark.

> **EXAMPLE** Does he play the drums well? [The sentence is a question, so it is followed by a question mark.]

EXERCISE A Decide whether each of the following is a statement or a question. Then, add the most appropriate punctuation mark where needed.

Example 1. We think it is cold in here. [The statement declares that we think it is cold, so the sentence is *declarative* and should be followed by a period.]

1. Did Jared forget his lunch [Should a period or a question mark follow this sentence?]

2. Have you washed and vacuumed the car

3. Debra is going to keep a snowball in her freezer

4. He wondered when the rain would stop

5. What did the puppy just do

11c. An exclamation (or exclamatory sentence) is followed by an exclamation point.

> **EXAMPLE** Wow, he sounds like a professional! [The sentence is an exclamation, so it is followed by an exclamation point.]

11d. A command or request (or imperative sentence) is followed by either a period or an exclamation point.

> **EXAMPLES** Please play your favorite jazz piece. [The sentence is a request, so it is followed by a period.]
>
> Stop littering now! [The sentence is a strong command, so it is followed by an exclamation point.]

EXERCISE B Decide whether each of the following is a statement, a question, an exclamation, or a command or request. Then, add the most appropriate punctuation mark where needed.

Example 1. We asked whether we could leave early. [The sentence makes a statement, so it should be followed by a period.]

6. What movie are you seeing tonight [Is this a statement about a movie, or is it asking a question?]

GO ON

7. Shoot the ball now

8. That concert was incredibly exciting

9. Please help me clear the table

10. She was wondering whether we would help move the sofa

Abbreviations

11e.   Use a period after certain abbreviations.

      EXAMPLES   George W. Bush [*W.* is an initial of *Walker*, a personal name, and is fol-
lowed by a period.]

                Sylvia Gonzalez, M.D. [*M.D.* is an abbreviation for *Medical Doctor*, an
academic degree, and is abbreviated using periods.]

                Phoenix, Ariz. [*Ariz.* is an abbreviation for *Arizona*, a geographical name,
and is followed by a period.]

EXERCISE C   Add periods where they are needed in each of the following word groups.

  Examples 1.   10:20 A.M. [The abbreviation of *ante meridiem* needs periods after each letter.]

          2.   Kenneth B. Gardner [The initial *B* should be followed by a period.]

11. Dr Truman [Does the abbreviation of *Doctor* need a period?]

12. J R R Tolkien [Do the initials in a name need periods?]

13. Mrs Jackson

14. Judy Stone, D D S

15. 108 West Oak St

16. Frank Salazar, Jr

17. San Diego, Calif

18. 1423 S First St

19. A D 1066

20. New York, N Y

Commas with Items in a Series

11f. Use commas to separate items in a series.

> **EXAMPLES** She has a collection of books, magazines, postcards, and letters. [Commas separate each item in the list of words within the sentence.]
>
> Did you look in the closet, on the desk, and under the sofa? [Each of the phrases within the question is a separate item, so commas separate them.]
>
> Houses and apartments make up the suburban core, inner-city businesses thrive, and commuters pack the freeways. [A comma separates the first two independent clauses of the list, and a comma followed by a coordinating conjunction separates the second and third independent clauses of the list.]

> **REMINDER▶** If all the items in a series are joined by *and, or,* or *nor,* commas are not needed to separate the items.
>
> **EXAMPLE** I will use pens **or** pencils **or** markers. [Because all items in the series are joined by *or,* no commas are needed to separate them.]

EXERCISE A Each of the following sentences contains items in a series. If the items require commas to separate them, insert commas where needed. If the items are already correctly punctuated, write *C* on the line provided.

Examples _____ **1.** We stood up, we clapped, and we cheered. [The three independent clauses should be separated by commas.]

_____*C*_____ **2.** Lakes and rivers and oceans help produce rain. [The conjunction *and* joins each item in the list, so the items should not be separated by commas.]

_____ **1.** Grandmother photographs family events prepares a scrapbook for each grandchild keeps a journal of vacation trips and attends most of our games. [Are the items in the list of Grandmother's activities clearly separated from each other?]

_____ **2.** Put the tomato plants the bags of mulch the hose and the small shovel into the wheelbarrow. [Is each item in the list of gardening supplies clearly separated from the next?]

_____ **3.** The musicians could be heard in the yard in the garden and throughout the house.

_____ **4.** Neither bees nor hornets nor wasps live in our attic.

_____ **5.** Alexandra Maria Kimi and Andrea are moving to new desks.

_____ **6.** Lightning flashed thunder boomed the wind howled and rain pelted the windows.

_____ **7.** Crickets will chirp rustle around in the dry leaves hop from corner to corner and sing through the night.

GO ON ▶

_____ **8.** Borrowing money or lending it or spending too much can cause financial woes.

_____ **9.** In the yard were four lawn chairs two tables and one open umbrella.

_____ **10.** I have cleaned the portable grill, Dan has packed the tent, and Lisa has made sand-

wiches and potato salad.

11f(3).   Use commas to separate two or more adjectives preceding a noun.

Do not use a comma between the last adjective in the series and the noun the adjectives modify.

> **EXAMPLE**   Sometimes I enjoy singing the driving, progressive, heartfelt songs from his
> new CD. [Commas separate each item in the series of adjectives preceding
> the noun *songs*, but there is no comma between *heartfelt* and *songs*.]

REMINDER Do not use a comma before the last adjective in a series if the adjective is part of a
compound noun.

> **EXAMPLE**   We'll hold the meeting in our large, comfortable living room. [No comma is
> needed to separate *comfortable* from *living* because *living room* is a
> compound noun.]

EXERCISE B Circle the letter of the sentence that is correctly punctuated in each of the following pairs.

Example 1. a. She lost a green, scuffed nylon wallet. [An additional comma is needed after

scuffed.]

(b.) This is a warm, well-lit, cheery dining room. [Two or more adjectives precede the

compound noun *dining room*, and commas separate each adjective.]

11. a. In which aisles can I find the dried, canned, and fresh beans?

b. Is this the shortest, quickest most direct route to Atlanta? [Which of the nouns, *beans* or *route*,

is preceded by two or more adjectives that are correctly separated by commas?]

12. a. Just look at the simple colorful, effective, scenery in that play.

b. We enjoyed the intense, dynamic, honest performance of the actor.

13. a. Yellow red, and green lights blinked around them.

b. Bring a large, yellow, ruled notepad to class.

14. a. Nate's thoughtful, artistic writing earned him many admirers.

b. He wrote short, deeply moving, stories.

15. a. Have you seen Josh's sturdy, lightweight mountain bike?

b. Lynn gave her sister a dark, blue, angora, sweater.

for **CHAPTER 11: PUNCTUATION**   *page 321*

Commas with Independent Clauses

11g. Use a comma before *and, but, for, nor, or, so,* or *yet* when the word joins independent clauses.

REMINDER An independent clause is a group of words that has a subject and verb. An independent clause also expresses a complete thought and can stand alone as a sentence.

    EXAMPLES   The teacher walked to the front of the classroom, and she smiled at the class. [A comma and the word *and* join the two independent clauses.]

                     Was she happy to be there, or was she nervous? [A comma and the word *or* join the question's two independent clauses.]

                     She had never taught language arts before, nor had she ever faced such a large group. [A comma and the word *nor* join the two independent clauses.]

EXERCISE A Circle the letter of the sentence that is punctuated correctly in each of the following pairs.

Example 1. a. Terrell has looked at stars before but he has never seen them through a telescope.

         (b.) For science, our group will write a research paper about astronomy, and we will also record our own observations. [A comma and the word *and* join the two independent clauses in sentence *b.*]

1. a. Shall we go to the library with Lou or shall we go stargazing tonight?

  b. The sky is clear enough for us to use your telescope, so we could start on our science project. [Which sentence contains two independent clauses joined by a comma and a coordinating conjunction?]

2. a. The skies were completely overcast earlier, but they are just partly cloudy now.

  b. There are some high, thin clouds but we can still see the moon and a few stars.

3. a. There are ice crystals in the thin clouds so there appears to be a ring around the moon.

  b. We can look at a few planets and stars, but we will not get a very clear view.

4. a. The clouds will not clear away tonight, nor will they clear by tomorrow night.

  b. We should postpone our project until the weekend for the weather will be better then.

5. a. Is your backyard a good location or can you think of a better place?

  b. We should take the telescope to the top of Mount Bonnell, for that location will give us an open view of the sky.

GO ON

NOTE Be careful not to confuse compound sentences with sentences containing compound verbs. A compound sentence contains two or more independent clauses, each of which has its own subject and verb. A sentence containing a compound verb usually has only one subject.

EXAMPLE Suddenly, the kitten raced from one end of the room to the other and then plopped down in the corner for a nap. [This sentence has two verbs, *raced* and *plopped*, but only one subject, *kitten*. This is not a compound sentence.]

EXERCISE B Each of the following sentences has one or two independent clauses. If the sentence is incorrectly punctuated, insert commas where they are needed. If the sentence is already correctly punctuated, write *C* on the line provided. Hint: Some sentences contain one independent clause with a compound verb.

Examples _____ **1.** Do you listen to music when you study, or do you prefer silence? [The two independent clauses are joined by the word *or*, so a comma must precede *or*.]

_____*C*_____ **2.** Some researchers are studying the effects of music and are finding links between music and memory. [The words *are studying* and *are finding* form a compound verb, so no comma is needed before the word *and*.]

_____ **6.** Most young adults enjoy music yet they dislike certain songs. [Do independent clauses both precede and follow the coordinating conjunction *yet*?]

_____ **7.** The right music may inspire and motivate people. [Are there two independent clauses in the sentence?]

_____ **8.** Many people can't sing well but they can play an instrument.

_____ **9.** Can music increase intelligence or aid creativity?

_____ **10.** Some students read and study better when listening to music.

_____ **11.** Vocal music may not help learning for the lyrics can interfere with concentration.

_____ **12.** Other students neither listen to the radio nor play CD's during study time.

_____ **13.** They enjoy music but they also find music distracting.

_____ **14.** Some classical music may improve test scores yet rock music can decrease them.

_____ **15.** Each person is different so you must choose your own study routine.

Commas with Introductory Elements

| **11i.** | Use a comma after certain introductory elements. |

EXAMPLES Well, it's your turn to wash the dishes. [A comma sets off the mild interjection *well* at the beginning of the statement.]

Smiling with relief, I jumped into the cool water. [A comma appears after the introductory participial phrase *Smiling with relief.*]

Next to the soap-filled sink, there were piles of dishes. [A comma appears after the long introductory prepositional phrase *Next to the soap-filled sink.*]

After we had finished drying the last glass, it was time put the dishes away. [A comma appears after the introductory adverb clause *After we had finished drying the last glass.*]

EXERCISE A Each of the following sentences contains either an introductory interjection or participial phrase. If the sentence is incorrectly punctuated, add commas where they are needed. If the sentence is already correctly punctuated, write *C* on the line provided.

Examples _____ **1.** Oh, I see your point. [The introductory interjection *Oh* must be set off from the rest of the sentence by a comma.]

___*C*___ **2.** Snoring like a chainsaw, I woke myself up. [A comma correctly sets off the introductory participial phrase *Snoring like a chainsaw* from the rest of the sentence.]

_____ **1.** Hey is that a dollar bill stuck to your shoe? [Is there an introductory interjection that needs a comma to set it apart from the rest of the sentence?]

_____ **2.** Swallowing nervously Carl wiped his sweaty hands on his jeans. [Does the sentence begin with a participial phrase that describes *Carl*?]

_____ **3.** Encouraged by the cheers of the fans, Reggie took his place on the pitcher's mound.

_____ **4.** My this has been an exciting first day.

_____ **5.** Raising her arms the vice-presidential nominee predicted victory.

_____ **6.** Sure there are a few bugs in the software program.

_____ **7.** Locked into our old views about eating how can we improve our diet?

_____ **8.** Well, maybe we should simply disband the committee altogether.

_____ **9.** Thinking of a dozen topics Wynnie couldn't decide where to begin her research.

_____ **10.** Yes isn't that the most interesting painting in the exhibit?

Other introductory elements include prepositional phrases and adverb clauses. Use a comma after two or more introductory prepositional phrases or after one long introductory prepositional phrase. Use a comma after an introductory adverb clause.

EXAMPLES   **At the store on the corner,** we can buy more apples. [The two introductory prepositional phrases *At the store* and *on the corner* are followed by a comma.]

After the long, dangerous migration south, the geese were exhausted. [The long introductory prepositional phrase *After the long, dangerous migration south* is followed by a comma.]

When the acorns fell from the trees, squirrels gathered and stored them. [The introductory adverb clause *When the acorns fell from the trees* is followed by a comma.]

EXERCISE B Each of the following sentences contains an introductory prepositional phrase or an introductory adverb clause. If the sentence is incorrectly punctuated, insert commas where they are needed. If the sentence is already correctly punctuated, write C on the line provided.

Examples _____ **1.** If you want to keep something safe, put it someplace no one will find it. [The introductory adverb clause *If you want to keep something safe* must be set off from the rest of the sentence by a comma.]

__C__ **2.** When I realized the importance of the papers, I decided to put them away. [The introductory adverb clause *When I realized the importance of the papers* is correctly set off from the rest of the sentence by a comma.]

_____**11.** Behind the poster of a buffalo you will find a wall safe. [Do two prepositional phrases introduce the sentence?]

_____**12.** Because it is strong, we keep our most valuable items inside the safe. [Does an adverb clause introduce the sentence?]

_____**13.** When it is locked the safe is almost impossible to crack.

_____**14.** In addition to that we can't forget where we've hidden the key.

_____**15.** After we searched the room, we discovered a great place in which to hide the key.

_____**16.** Although our sister didn't like the choice we knew what to do.

_____**17.** Since we didn't want to forget where we hid it we decided to keep the key nearby.

_____**18.** Against our sister's repeated advice we hid the key on the back of the poster.

_____**19.** With all of her objections you'd think that we'd left the key in plain sight.

_____**20.** If she doesn't understand our reasoning about hiding places she can hide her valuables somewhere else.

Commas with Interrupters

11j. Use commas to set off elements that interrupt the sentence.

EXAMPLES   Emily Dickinson, the poet, says that hope has feathers. [Commas set off the phrase *the poet* from the rest of the sentence. Since the sentence means the same thing without the phrase, the phrase is nonessential.]

What do you think she meant, Eric? [One comma sets off the name *Eric,* which is used in direct address at the end of the sentence.]

In my opinion, she probably meant that hope has qualities similar to those of a bird. [One comma sets off the parenthetical expression *In my opinion* from the rest of the sentence.]

EXERCISE A Circle the letter of the sentence that is correctly punctuated in each of the following pairs.

Example 1. ⓐ Flash, a Shetland sheepdog, is my favorite dog.

    b. Nicole my neighbor, is my closest friend. [Commas should appear before and after nonessential information.]

1. a. A large SUV I believe, uses far more fuel than a large car.

    b. A small car, on the other hand, is usually the most fuel-efficient of all. [Does one word group have a parenthetical comment set off by commas?]

2. a. You're right Rudy, you are next in line.

    b. We need to load up the picnic supplies, David. [Does one group of words contain a name used in direct address correctly set off by a comma or commas?]

3. a. This air conditioner, a Kool-Aire, is the most energy-efficient model on the market.

    b. My teacher Ms. Brown, assigned an essay on civil rights.

4. a. Long-distance runners according to sports medicine doctors, should watch their diets.

    b. The house, nevertheless, needs to be painted.

5. a. The big black bear, a handsome example of the animal, rose on his hind legs.

    b. Why won't Tom, the karate instructor offer more classes after school?

6. a. Tomorrow according to the weather forecaster will be sunny and hot.

    b. This soup, in my opinion, needs more garlic.

7. a. I'm already on my way, Cheryl.

    b. Reuben what time do you think we should leave for San Antonio?

8. a. Alicia's cousin, Marlene, has five sisters.

    b. The bluejay a noisy and aggressive bird chased the other birds from the feeder.

9. a. We will arrive at our first stop on the tour, Cairo about 10:00 Tuesday morning.

   b. The Egyptian pyramids, one of the Seven Wonders of the World, are breathtaking.

10. a. Ms. Johnson's car, a red sports car, is in the shop for repair.

   b. My mother Mrs. Gibson works as a chemical engineer.

REMINDER Information essential to the meaning of the sentence should not be set apart by commas.

> **EXAMPLE** We will read Emily Dickinson's poem "A Narrow Fellow in the Grass" for tomorrow's assignment. [No commas set off *"A Narrow Fellow in the Grass"* because Dickinson wrote many poems. The title is needed to identify which poem has been assigned, so the information is essential.]

EXERCISE B Read each of the following sentences containing interrupters. If the sentence is incorrectly punctuated, insert commas where they are needed. If the sentence is already correctly punctuated, write *C* on the line provided.

Examples _____ **1.** Robert, you'd better slow down. [The name *Robert* is used in direct address, so a comma must set it apart from the rest of the sentence.]

___*C*___ **2.** My neighbor Mr. Murphy is building a boat. [No commas set off the name *Mr. Murphy* because the speaker has more than one neighbor. Mr. Murphy's name is needed to identify him.]

_____ **11.** Recycling, generally speaking is good for the environment. [Does the sentence contain a parenthetical phrase that needs a second comma to fully set it off from the rest of the sentence?]

_____ **12.** Could this be a case of mistaken identity Maria? [Does the question include a name used in direct address?]

_____ **13.** My cat Smudge, would never have climbed into Dad's new car.

_____ **14.** That nevertheless is exactly where I found him.

_____ **15.** Pablo Picasso, the world-renowned artist still has thousands of admirers today.

_____ **16.** The game consequently will have to be rescheduled.

_____ **17.** Moreover, the dramatic lighting adds to the sense of danger.

_____ **18.** Have you computed the figures, Ellen, for the final report?

_____ **19.** According to the survey in the *Sun Times* our only newspaper the election will be very close.

_____ **20.** My friend Elena will vacation in Montana this summer.

Semicolons

Use a semicolon between independent clauses that are closely related in meaning if they are not joined by *and, but, for, nor, or, so,* or *yet,* and between independent clauses joined by a conjunctive adverb or transitional expression.

> **EXAMPLES**   We found the missing calculator; it was under a sofa cushion. [A semicolon joins the two closely related independent clauses.]
>
> Her shoelace snapped; therefore, her shoe flew off. [A semicolon appears between two independent clauses joined by a conjunctive adverb.]

REMINDER *Conjunctive adverbs* and *transitional expressions* show readers how linked independent clauses are related to each other.

EXERCISE A Each of the following sentences contains two independent clauses. If the sentence is punctuated incorrectly, circle the punctuation mark that should be replaced by a semicolon. If the sentence is punctuated correctly, write *C* on the line provided.

Examples _____ **1.** Some counties are huge, Los Angeles County covers 4,083 square miles of city, island, desert, and seacoast. [A semicolon should join the two closely related independent clauses.]

_____ **2.** It's begun to rain, still, the dog wants to go outside. [A semicolon should precede the conjunctive adverb *still.*]

_____ **1.** The western sky has reddened, the sun will set within the hour. [Should the independent clauses be joined by a semicolon?]

_____ **2.** Beth has finished assembling her solar lawn mower, however, the blades still need to be balanced. [Should a semicolon precede the conjunctive adverb in this sentence?]

_____ **3.** It is getting easier to find many forms of wildlife, indeed, even the bald eagle is becoming more common.

_____ **4.** Her aunt gave her some potted violets, so she is learning how to grow them.

_____ **5.** He's eating fresh cantaloupe, where did he find it?

_____ **6.** There are empty boxes stacked in the hallway, we should probably recycle them.

_____ **7.** Comets are difficult to discover, yet Dr. Rhodes keeps trying to find one.

_____ **8.** Carl's books, papers, and pencils are already lying on the table in the kitchen, in other words, our study group is probably going to meet there.

_____ **9.** To reach the doctor's office, go to the fourth floor, the office will be on your left.

_____ **10.** The bridge is usually busy with traffic, nevertheless, pigeons nest below it.

GO ON

Use a semicolon between items in a series if the items contain commas. A semicolon, rather than a comma, also may be needed to separate independent clauses joined by a coordinating conjunction when the clauses contain commas that may be confusing.

EXAMPLES   Turn in the assignment, your math homework; the art project, if you've finished it; and the final draft of your persuasive essay. [The first two items in this series contain commas, so semicolons separate all the items.]

Ice, lettuce, bread, and drinks should fit inside the chest; and the tent, sleeping bags, and clothes should fit inside the pack. [The two independent clauses contain commas that may be confusing, so they are joined by a semicolon and the coordinating conjunction *and*.]

EXERCISE B Each of the following sentences contains either two independent clauses or a list of items. If the sentence is punctuated incorrectly, circle the punctuation mark that should be replaced by a semicolon. If the sentence is punctuated correctly, write *C* on the line provided.

Example _____ **1.** We know that the tubas, as old, dented, and rusted as they are, have to be replaced, but the trumpets, which are fairly new, well cared for, and shiny, can be kept. [The coordinating conjunction *but* joins two independent clauses containing commas; therefore, a semicolon joins them.]

_____ **11.** Unlike nonliving things, living things move on their own, respond to changes in condition, consume nutrients, and grow and replace parts. [Do the items in the list contain commas that may confuse a reader?]

_____ **12.** On their whirlwind tour of the East, the retirees will visit Orlando, Florida, Richmond, Virginia, and Boston, Massachusetts.

_____ **13.** Three of Oklahoma's natural regions are the Gulf Coastal Plain, a fertile region that spreads along the valley of the Red River, the Ouachita Mountains, a forested area that extends into western Arkansas, and the Central Plains, a grassland prairie that forms the largest region in the state.

_____ **14.** A spokesperson for the San Gabriel Community Center said that they can host the "Build a Better Mousetrap" competition on November 16 or 23, 2009, December 12 or 29, 2009, January 6 or 23, 2010, or February 9 or 16, 2010.

_____ **15.** Artificial turf doesn't require much care, isn't easily damaged, and is unaffected by weather, but its use may lead to certain injuries, cause balls to bounce higher than they would on a natural surface, and raise field temperatures in warm weather.

Colons

Use a colon to mean "note what follows" before a list of items, before a long, formal statement or quotation, and between independent clauses when the second clause explains or restates the ideas of the first.

EXAMPLES   You will need the following supplies: a rubber band, two paper clips, a pencil, and one wooden toothpick. [The colon announces that the sentence includes a list of items that should be noted.]

Mayor Castleton proclaimed this: "Today, we celebrate the opening of the city's newest middle school. Next month, we will celebrate the opening of our largest city park. Within five years we will have built two more schools, two more parks, and a public pool. If that doesn't spell civilization, I must not be able to spell!" [The colon precedes a long, formal quotation, and, because it starts with a complete sentence, the quotation begins with a capital letter.]

Her parents overcame much adversity: They had grown up in poverty, traveled across an ocean, and started a business from scratch. [The second independent clause explains the idea of the first clause, and, because it is a complete sentence, the second clause begins with a capital letter.]

EXERCISE A   Use proofreading symbols to correct any incorrect punctuation and to insert correct punctuation where needed in the following sentences. Remember to change capitalization when needed.

Example 1. The station was noisy; adults chatted loudly, children laughed and yelled, and the subway trains occasionally came roaring to a stop. [Because the second independent clause explains the idea of the first clause and is a complete sentence, a colon should separate them and the second clause should begin with a capital letter.]

1. Do not forget to bring the following materials; entry fees, all photographs and artwork, display stands, a display table, a comfortable chair or stool, a list of prices for any artwork offered for sale, and a calculator. [Should a colon follow *materials*?]

2. Our treasurer reminded us. "we must act before it is too late. We must respond to the demands of the current situation. If we are to avoid a financial crisis that might put us out of business altogether, all new members need to get their dues in to their team leaders within two days."

Developmental Language Skills

3. We will need these supplies, six fresh cans of paint, three paintbrushes, two paint rollers, a pair of paint trays, a protective sheet, a small ladder, masking tape, and old clothes.

4. Additional recommendations are as follows, decrease expenses and levels of absenteeism, and improve production efficiencies and levels of sales.

5. In a speech delivered to this year's graduates, she said, "the diploma you'll receive today is far more than a piece of paper. It is, instead, a symbol of triumph. It is a symbol of determination and dedication to success. Indeed, when you finally hold the diploma you are about to receive, remember that it is not a piece of paper. It is a flag you are receiving. A flag dedicated to victory."

Colons are also used in certain conventional situations. Use a colon between the hour and minute, between chapter and verse in Biblical references, between titles and subtitles, and after the salutation of a business letter.

> **EXAMPLES**   12:47 P.M. [The colon separates hours from minutes.]
> Genesis 1:4–12 [The colon separates chapter and verse in a Biblical reference]
> *The Restful Hour:Teatime in Literary England* [A colon separates title and subtitle.]
> To Whom It May Concern: [A colon is used after the salutation of a business letter.]

EXERCISE B For each of the following groups of words, use proofreading symbols to insert correct punctuation or to replace incorrect punctuation where needed.

Example 1. Matthew 6:2 contains a brief lesson in selflessness. [A colon separates chapter and verse in Biblical references.]

6. Sometime between 8 16 A.M. and 8 19 A.M. teachers will announce the results of last week's election.

7. *Elements of Literature—Third Course*

8. Pharaoh's daughter, in Exodus 2;6, feels sorry for the baby she's found.

9. Our flight departs at 5–55 A.M.

10. Dear Dr. Delgado,

Italics (Underlining)

Titles and Subtitles

13a. Use italics (underlining) for titles and subtitles of books, periodicals, long poems, plays, films, television series, long musical works and recordings, and works of art.

BOOK	*The Moon Smiled: New Folk Tales*	**FILM**	*Help!*
PERIODICAL	*The Sciences*	**TELEVISION SERIES**	*Mystery!*
LONG POEM	*Paradise Lost*	**LONG MUSICAL WORK**	*Messiah*
PLAY	*The Miracle Worker*	**WORK OF ART**	*St. Stephen*

EXERCISE A Underline the word or words that should be italicized in each of the following sentences.

Examples 1. <u>Life and Times of Frederick Douglass</u> is a great book! [The book title *Life and Times of Frederick Douglass* should be italicized (underlined).]

2. Was <u>Parsifal</u> the last of Richard Wagner's operas? [The title of the long musical work *Parsifal* should be italicized (underlined).]

1. Has Jane Austen's book Pride and Prejudice ever been made into a movie? [Does this question contain a book's title that needs to be italicized (underlined)?]

2. One of Donatello's marble sculptures, St. George, depicts human self-confidence. [Does this sentence contain a work of art's title that needs to be italicized (underlined)?]

3. William Shakespeare wrote Romeo and Juliet.

4. Someone sent a long letter to The Middlevale Gazette saying that its editorials were too long.

5. We have a recording of Amahl and the Night Visitors, the first opera written for television.

6. The movie Apollo 13 is about events that happened before I was born.

7. No one knows who wrote Beowulf, the epic poem.

8. Georgia O'Keeffe's artistic style is displayed in her painting Black Iris.

9. Dr. Seuss once worked as an illustrator and humorist for the magazine Life.

10. Some of Nathaniel Hawthorne's stories were collected in the book Twice-Told Tales.

Names

13b. Use italics (underlining) for the names of ships, trains, aircraft, and spacecraft.

SHIP	*Pequod*	**AIRCRAFT**	*Spruce Goose*
TRAIN	*General*	**SPACECRAFT**	*Galileo*

GO ON

EXERCISE B Underline the word or words that should be italicized in each of the following sentences.

Example 1. Arturo says that if he ever buys an ocean liner he's going to name it Idler. [Because it is the name of a ship, *Idler* is italicized (underlined).]

11. My parents once got up early enough to see the space station Mir pass overhead. [Has the name of the spacecraft been underlined?]

12. Paul is fascinated with the battle between Merrimack and Monitor, two ironclad ships used during the Civil War.

13. Didn't the first U.S. space satellite, Explorer 1, discover charged particles surrounding Earth?

14. Like several other lighter-than-air aircraft, the Shenandoah couldn't withstand poor weather.

15. The Chisholms aren't here because they're taking a train trip aboard the Kentucky Flyer.

Words, Letters, Symbols, and Numerals

13c. Use italics (underlining) for words, letters, symbols and numerals referred to as such and for foreign words that are not yet a part of the English vocabulary.

> **EXAMPLES** How many *l's* are in the word ***parallel?*** [Both the letter *l* and the word *parallel* are referred to as such and are italicized (underlined).]
>
> Add an @ and a **7** to the e-mail address. [Both the symbol @ and the numeral 7 are referred to as such and have been underlined (italicized).]
>
> In Spanish, a volleyball is called a ***voley-playa.*** [*Voley-playa* is not part of English vocabulary, so it is italicized (underlined).]

EXERCISE C Underline the words, symbols, letters, or numerals that should be italicized in the following sentences.

Example 1. It looks like he added a % after the 18. [The symbol % and the numeral *18* are referred to as such, so both should be italicized (underlined).]

16. She told him not to worry because it was only an igel, or, as she explained, a hedgehog. [Which foreign word needs to be italicized (underlined) in the sentence?]

17. Be certain to use the ¶ mark to indicate where your paragraphs should begin.

18. In French, the two words for "personal computer" are ordinateur personnel.

19. His handwriting is hard to read, but it looks like he wrote down a 93 as his best golf score.

20. The £ symbol looks odd to us, but it stands for "pound," an English unit of currency.

Quotation Marks A

Direct Quotations

13d. Use quotation marks to enclose a *direct quotation*—a person's exact words.

13e. A direct quotation generally begins with a capital letter.

EXAMPLES "This is blocked," he said. [Quotation marks begin and end his exact words.]

Raul laughed, "We'd better try a different hallway." [Quotation marks precede and follow Raul's words, and the quotation begins with a capital letter.]

EXERCISE A Insert quotation marks where they are needed, and draw three lines under any letters that should be capitalized in each of the following sentences containing direct quotations.

Examples 1. According to Paul, "bees are best left alone." [Paul's quoted sentence should begin with a capital letter and should end with a quotation mark.]

2. Sarah said, "don't peel that orange. We need to save it for later." [Sarah's quotation should both begin and end with quotation marks, and the quotation should begin with a capital letter.]

1. Hold on a minute! Lani hollered. [Do quotation marks clearly tell a reader where Lani's exact words begin and end?]

2. The electrician said, go ahead and flip the circuit breakers back on.

3. "Do you think we can climb over all of those hills in just one afternoon? said Audrey.

4. Jesse grabbed a sweater, swung the walk-in cooler's door open, and mumbled, it's chilly in there.

5. She explained, you'll get there if you turn right on Bleaker and then walk one block.

6. Rosa wondered aloud, Should I go upstairs or stay down here?"

7. I can't go. You know I have to visit my cousins, Crystal told us.

8. Run to second base! yelled the coach.

9. I heard someone shout, "don't forget to close the door!"

10. can you believe this weather?" Len asked with a smile.

GO ON

If an interrupting expression divides a quoted sentence into two parts, the second part of the quoted sentence begins with a lowercase letter. When a sentence continues after a direct quotation ends, the direct quotation may end in a comma, a question mark, or an exclamation point, but not in a period.

EXAMPLES "Well," the manager smiled, "sales have skyrocketed this month." [An expression, *the manager smiled*, interrupts the quoted sentence, so the final part of the sentence begins with a lowercase letter.]
Hester wondered, "Should we leave the broken chair?" once we'd finished loading the truck. [Although the sentence continues after the direct quotation has ended, Hester's words end in a question mark.]

EXERCISE B Read each of the following sentences containing direct quotations. Insert quotation marks where they are needed. Then, use proofreaders' marks to correct any errors in capitalization or punctuation.

Examples 1. "Can we please," Erica frowned at the television, "Do something else?" [Quotation marks should enclose each portion of Erica's direct quotation, and the portion of her quoted sentence that follows an interrupting expression should begin with a lowercase letter.]

2. Lian asked, "when are you going to write that letter?" [Quotation marks should begin and end Lian's exact words and her quoted sentence should begin with a capital letter.]

11. "I think I'd rather be walking, she said, than waiting to go for a walk." [Is each portion of her direct quotation set off from the rest of the sentence by quotation marks?]

12. "The only problem," he grinned, is that we don't have a car. [Is each portion of his direct quotation set off from the rest of the sentence by quotation marks?]

13. "Little man, always be polite! My grandmother used to say.

14. "All leaders should line up at noon, the memo read, So don't be late!

15. Step right up, the carnival worker teased, And try your luck!

16. She wondered, is this the only map we have? as she gazed at the tattered page.

17. The coach bellowed, Listen up! once the team was seated.

18. "I," he sighed beside us on the plane, hear a baby cooing in the seats behind us."

19. Your curiosity, Ms. Carvel whispered to her daughters, "is a gift."

20. "We have a guest, our teacher told us, "Visiting this morning."

Quotation Marks B

Titles

13l. Use quotation marks to enclose titles and subtitles of articles, essays, short stories, poems, songs, individual episodes of TV series, and chapters and other parts of books and periodicals.

ARTICLE	"Boldly Going, Going, Going . . ."
ESSAY	"Buffalo Sun: Prairie Ecosystems"
SONG	"America"
POEM	"Gold"
TV EPISODE	"Winter Chill"
BOOK CHAPTER	"The Garden"
SHORT STORY	"Twyla"

EXERCISE A Where needed, insert quotation marks around the titles of essays, short stories, poems, songs, television episodes, or book chapters in each of the following sentences.

Examples 1. What rhythms in Edna St. Vincent Millay's poem "The Courage That My Mother Had" can you identify? [The title of a poem should be enclosed by quotation marks.]

        2. In his article "Piltdown Unmasked" author Phillip V. Tobias provides a history of a famous scientific hoax. [The title of an article should be enclosed by quotation marks.]

1. In his article How Insects Learned to Fly, James H. Marden discusses early insects and how they first began to fly. [Does the sentence contain an article's title that should be enclosed by quotation marks?]

2. His grandfather is always whistling the chorus to the song When I'm Sixty Four. [Does the sentence contain a song's title that should be enclosed by quotation marks?]

3. Her parents first fell in love when they both agreed that The Trouble with Tribbles was the best episode of that old show.

4. In English class, we've been talking about Guy de Maupassant's short story The Necklace.

5. Is The Washwoman a first-person short story, or is it an autobiographical essay?

6. On the bus, her brother and his friends sang The Ants Go Marching for most of the day.

7. The poem The Lesson of the Moth is supposed to have been written by a cockroach.

8. I'm sure that she said to read the chapter Sharing an Opinion.

GO ON

9. Believe it or not, after following the instructions in the chapter Using Brochures, Jody created a

brochure that convinced his parents to take a family vacation.

10. Roald Dahl's story about a man who thinks that a snake is sleeping on his stomach, Poison, is

really an attack on racist thinking.

EXERCISE B Write a title on each of the lines provided that corresponds to the noun underlined in the
sentence. Be sure to use quotation marks correctly where needed. You can make up the names for any
titles you may need.

Examples 1. My big sister says that _____"Thank You M'am"_____ is the best short story ever

written. [Because it is the title of a short story, "Thank You M'am" should be enclosed by

quotation marks.]

2. According to this article, _____"Mother Nature's Little Fits"_____, we're in for some nasty

weather this winter. [Because it is a title in a periodical, "Mother Nature's Little Fits"

should be enclosed by quotation marks.]

11. _____ is a poem suited to the discussions we've been having.

[Have you included quotation marks around the title of the poem you've chosen?]

12. I've already finished reading _____, which is a chapter in our text-

book. [Have you included quotation marks around the title of the textbook chapter you've chosen?]

13. We really enjoyed the article titled _____.

14. How in the world did you memorize the poem _____ so quickly?

15. _____ is a short story meant to tell us a great deal about the central

character's strengths.

16. The essay _____ encourages people to take a positive view of the

future.

17. Have you heard the song _____ yet?

18. On the Internet, I found an article called _____ about subway

systems.

19. Tonight's television episode, _____, will surely draw a large

audience.

20. Have any of you read the short story _____?

Apostrophes
Possessive Case

14a. To form the possessive case of most singular nouns, add an apostrophe and an *s*.

> **EXAMPLE**   Can we take a look at this **month's** calendar? [*Month* is a singular noun. An apostrophe and *s* form the possessive.]

> **NOTE** If a proper name ending in *s* has two or more syllables and if the addition of an apostrophe and *s* will make the name awkward to pronounce, add only the apostrophe.

> **EXAMPLE**   Wyatt is looking forward to reading about **Odysseus'** adventures. [*Odysseus* is a four-syllable name ending in *s*. Adding an apostrophe and *s* will make the name awkward to pronounce (O-dys-se-us-es).]

EXERCISE A   For the following sentences, create the possessive case for each underlined noun by using proofreading symbols to add an apostrophe or apostrophe and *s* as needed.

Example 1.   The lab has yet to identify the gas's properties. [The possessive of this singular noun takes an apostrophe and *s*.]

1. Penicillin discovery was almost a matter of luck. [Are both an apostrophe and an *s* needed to create the possessive case of this noun?]

2. One of Lampasas (pronounced "Lam-pass-us") attractions is a set of mineral springs.

3. Because he wasn't looking while he poured, Kito's juice overflowed the glass rim.

4. Isn't that bag full of Mr. Bedford laundry?

5. Look at the size of that hippopotamus jaw!

> When plural nouns end in *s*, form the possessive case by adding an apostrophe alone, but to form the possessive case of plural nouns that do not end in *s*, add both an apostrophe and an *s*. Add both an apostrophe and an *s* to certain indefinite pronouns, and never add an apostrophe to a possessive personal pronoun.

> **EXAMPLES**   Where are the **wheels'** lug nuts? [*Wheels* is a plural noun ending in *s*, so an apostrophe alone is added.]

> The surface of the floor in the **men's** gymnasium has been refinished. [*Men* is a plural noun that does not end in *s*, so an apostrophe and *s* are added.]

> Lita returned **someone's** lost keys to the office. [*Someone* is an indefinite pronoun, so an apostrophe and *s* are added.]

> **Its** nest is near **your** home. [*Its* and *your* are possessive personal pronouns.]

GO ON ➡

Developmental Language Skills

EXERCISE B Underline the word in each set of parentheses in the following sentences that is the correct form of the possessive case of that word.

Example 1. On (*someones'*, *someone's*) advice, she visited her (*cousins'*, *cousins's*) school. [*Someone* takes an apostrophe and an *s*, while *cousins* takes an apostrophe alone.]

6. Make sure our (*bosses'*, *bosses's*) files get put into the cabinet that is (*theirs*, *their's*). [Is *bosses* a plural noun ending in *s*? Does a possessive personal pronoun take an apostrophe?]

7. The (*herons'*, *herons's*) squawking convinced a frog to dive from (*it's*, *its*) rock.

8. When the (*womens'*, *women's*) two children got home, (*neithers'*, *neither's*) shoes were on.

9. Are these (*ties'*, *tie's*) colors (*his*, *his'*) best choice to go with those shirts?

10. The (*delegates's*, *delegates'*) conservation proposal gained (*everyone's*, *everyones'*) approval.

Contractions and Plurals

14g. Use an apostrophe to show where letters, numerals, or words have been omitted in a contraction.

> **EXAMPLES** we + have = we've   should + not = shouldn't
> of + the + clock = o'clock   1957 − 1900 = '57

14h. To prevent confusion, use an apostrophe and an *s* to form the plurals of lowercase letters, some capital letters, numerals, symbols, and some words that are referred to as words.

> **EXAMPLES** There are four *s*'s in the word *Mississippi*. [The letter *s* is lowercase, so its plural is formed by adding an apostrophe and *s* in roman type.]
> *U*'s go in the first column. [Without an apostrophe, *U* might look like *Us*, so its plural is formed by adding an apostrophe and *s* in roman type.]
> Do we use @'s and *&*'s in the report? [@ and *&* are symbols, so each plural is formed by adding an apostrophe and *s* in roman type.]

EXERCISE C For each of the following sentences, insert apostrophes where necessary.

Example 1. Ralph won't tell me what these little *'s in his note mean! [*Won't* is a contraction of *will* and *not*, and *'s is the plural of a symbol.]

11. Shouldnt we tell them that theyre supposed to use *as* and *bs* rather than *1s* and *2s* in their outlines? [Have you added apostrophes to the contractions and plurals of letters and numerals?]

12. Mikes agreeing that hed prefer to get to class at nine oclock.

13. Youre definitely going to get *As* if your study habits dont change.

14. Back in 49, after studying this creek, she predicted that wed eventually discover gold here.

15. If we are going to finish this project on time, its easy to see that were going to need to remove some of the *donts* and *wonts* from our vocabularies.

Hyphens and Ellipses

Hyphens

15a. Use hyphens to divide a word at the end of a line.

> **EXAMPLE** An arctic front is almost certain to reach us by tomorrow morn-
> ing. [A hyphen is used to divide the word *morning* at the end of the line.]

NOTE Divide words between syllables, between prefixes and suffixes and their base words, or, if a word is already hyphenated, only at the hyphen. Do not divide a word so that one letter stands alone.

> **EXAMPLES** Por-tu-gal [between syllables] in-born [between prefix and base]
> tire-less [between base and suffix] one-track [already hyphenated]

EXERCISE A Use a dictionary to determine where each underlined word might be divided. Then, on the line provided, write the hyphenated word. If a word cannot be hyphenated, write *C*.

Example _____*C*_____ **1.** The store is <u>open</u> today. [*Open* cannot be divided because the letter *o* would be left standing alone.]

_____ **1.** The book concerns politics in <u>Nepal</u>. [Can *Nepal* be hyphenated?]

_____ **2.** Coretta wants to write "hit" <u>Broadway</u> plays.

_____ **3.** Chad's desire to stay in shape <u>stopped</u> him from ordering dessert.

_____ **4.** Has the back door been left <u>ajar</u> again?

_____ **5.** I've never seen a <u>holograph</u> that looked very realistic.

Use hyphens with the following: compound numbers from twenty-one to ninety-nine; fractions used as modifiers; the prefixes *ex–, self–, all–,* and *great–;* the suffixes *–elect* and *–free;* prefixes before proper nouns or adjectives; and with compound adjectives that precede the nouns they modify.

> **EXAMPLES** sixty-one [*Sixty-one* is a compound number from twenty-one to ninety-nine.]
> one-quarter turn [*One-quarter* is an adjective modifying *turn.*]
> all-powerful [*All-powerful* contains the prefix *all.*]
> drug-free [*Drug-free* contains the suffix *free.*]
> pre-Columbian [*Pre-Columbian* contains a prefix before a proper noun.]
> one-of-a-kind park [*One-of-a-kind* is a compound adjective preceding a noun.]

EXERCISE B Read the following sentences to determine which words need to be hyphenated. Then, use proofreading symbols to insert hyphens where needed.

Example 1. This park is now a litter free zone. [The suffix *–free* should be hyphenated.]

GO ON

6. The formula calls for one half ounce acetic acid. [Does a fraction modify a noun in this sentence?]

7. Tyrone's score on this game may be an all time high.

8. Some preSocratic philosophers thought the universe was made of water.

9. At least forty five bearings are inside this wheel's hub.

10. Isn't she an exmember of the debating team?

Ellipses

15h. Use ellipsis points (. . .) to mark omissions from quoted materials.

> **ORIGINAL**   The only road she ever wandered, **despite what you may hear,** was her own.
>
> **QUOTED**   According to Ethel's biographer, "The only road she ever wandered . . . was her own." [Three spaced ellipsis points indicate that the middle of the sentence has been omitted.]

NOTE To omit words at the end of a sentence within quotation marks, keep the sentence's end punctuation and follow it with three spaced ellipsis points.

> **ORIGINAL**   The longest structure ever built is the Great Wall, which was constructed by hand.
>
> **QUOTED**   The author writes, "The longest structure ever built is the Great Wall. . . ." [A period followed by three spaced ellipsis points indicates that the end of the sentence has been omitted.]

EXERCISE C Omit the underlined phrases and sentences in the following items. Insert ellipses where they are needed, placing #'s where spaces should appear.

Example 1. The sun ~~rose slowly and~~ peeped between our blinds. [The ellipsis stands in for the

#.#.#.#

omitted words *rose slowly and,* and spaces appear between the points.]

11. The center stands on three acres of woodland, and it houses sixteen injured birds. [Have you

inserted an ellipsis and indicated where spaces should be?]

12. People often find downed birds and bring them to the center.

13. Our biggest success was with a golden eagle that we released this fall.

14. Her first fuzz-covered eaglet has just hatched.

15. It's almost ready to fly alongside its parents and other eagles because its regular feathers have

begun to grow.

Parentheses, Dashes, and Brackets

Parentheses

15e. Use parentheses to enclose material that is added to a sentence but is not considered to be of major importance.

> **EXAMPLE** In the United States, Elizabeth Cady Stanton **(**1815–1902**)** helped establish a woman's right to vote. [The dates tell when Ms. Stanton was born and when she died. They are in parentheses because they may be useful additional information, but they are not important to the sentence's main idea.]

EXERCISE A Determine the main idea of each of the following sentences. Then, set off any additional unimportant material by inserting parentheses where needed. Do not add commas.

Example 1. Wolverines weigh up to fifty-five pounds (twenty-five kilograms) and are now rare. [The words *twenty-five kilograms* add useful information to the sentence, but they are unimportant to its main idea, so they appear within parentheses.]

1. The Empire State Building located on Fifth Avenue was completed in 1931. [Which information is both additional and unimportant to the main idea of this sentence?]

2. George Eliot 1819–1880 is the pen name of the novelist Mary Ann Evans.

3. By December 15, 1791, the Bill of Rights the first ten amendments to the Constitution had been approved by a sufficient number of states.

4. Mark Twain Samuel Langhorne Clemens wrote *Life on the Mississippi.*

5. *When I Was Young in the Mountains* 1982 is a book about Cynthia Rylant's childhood in West Virginia.

Dashes

15f. Use a dash to indicate an abrupt break in thought or speech or an unfinished statement or question.

> **EXAMPLE** "Don't you think that cleaning up will be—" Carmen began, and then she paused to reconsider. [The dash indicates that Carmen's question remains unfinished.]

15g. Use a dash to indicate *namely, that is,* or *in other words* or to otherwise introduce an explanation.

> **EXAMPLE** Brushes, cans of paint, dropcloths, and scrapers—these are the tools of my trade! [The dash indicates **namely** *the brushes, cans of paint, drop cloths, and scrapers.*]

GO ON

EXERCISE B Insert dashes that indicate breaks in thought, *namely, that is, in other words,* or introduce an explanation in each of the following sentences. Do not add commas.

Example 1. Certain birds ͜ cardinals and mockingbirds ͜ build their nests in shrubs or low trees. [The dashes indicate *that is* cardinals and mockingbirds.]

6. Their ancestral homes small mud and straw buildings eroded into dust long ago. [Have you used dashes to set off an explanation from the rest of the sentence?]

7. Sheila's little sister she's only seven years old is already studying algebra.

8. The Aztecs' principal food consisted of cornmeal pancakes tortillas.

9. "So when is this roller coaster going to take" he said, and then he shrieked.

10. The Taj Mahal one of the most expensive tombs ever built was constructed in memory of an Indian ruler's wife.

Brackets

15i. Use brackets to enclose an explanation within quoted or parenthetical material.

> **EXAMPLE** Dr. Thomas writes, "We found it **[the serving bowl]** after only two days of digging." [*The serving bowl* appears within brackets because it is an explanation of quoted material and is not a part of the original quotation.]

EXERCISE C Fill in the blanks with short explanations that correspond to the words found in parentheses at the end of each of the following sentences. You can make up any explanations you need.

Example 1. Our research indicates that the lake's aquatic life is continuing to diversify. (See Appendix A ___[439]___.) *(a page number)* [Because explanatory information, *439*, has been included within parenthetical material, brackets enclose the information.]

11. The Board of Directors announced, "We are happy that all of our new stores will be operational soon _____, and we are pleased by increased growth." *(the name of a month)*

12. "The main character _____ often agrees with the nation's value system," he explained. *(a character's name)*

13. "While we all knew who would win the student assembly seat _____, we hadn't expected it to be by such a large margin." *(the name of the winner)*

14. I hope that this letter (and the enclosed materials _____) have arrived safely. *(a description of the enclosed materials)*

15. He tells us, "According to her book, they _____ have never been seen alive in their deep-sea home." *(a type of sea animal)*

Words with *ie* and *ei*

16b. Write *ie* when the sound is long *e*, except after *c*.

The long *e* sound is what you hear in words such as *chief*, *heat*, and *deep*.

EXAMPLES	*i* before *e*:	*ei* after *c*:
	achieve	ceiling
	believe	conceit
	brief	deceit
	grief	perceive
	shield	receive
	yield	

16c. Write *ei* when the sound is not long *e*, especially when the sound is long *a*.

The long *a* sound is what you hear in words such as *bake*, *late*, and *say*.

EXAMPLES	*ei*:	*ei* pronounced *ay*:
	forfeit	neighbor
	foreign	freight
	height	weight
	heir	sleigh
		vein

TIP If you are having trouble with the above guidelines, it is always good to remember the old rhyme: **i** *before* **e,** *except after* **c** *(or when pronounced* **ay,** *as in* neighbor *and* weigh.)

EXERCISE A Underline the word in parentheses that is spelled correctly in each of the following sentences.

Examples 1. Load that piano into the *(frieght, freight)* elevator. [The letters are pronounced *ay*. The correct spelling is *freight*.]

2. There is a difference between being *(conceited, concieted)* and being proud of yourself for a job well done. [The letters make a long *e* sound, and they follow *c*. The correct spelling is *conceited*.]

1. The dark suit, sunglasses, and calm smile made her appear to be a master of *(deciet, deceit)*. [Do the letters make a long *e* sound? Do they follow *c*?]

2. My older brother is very nervous about his upcoming job *(interview, interveiw)*. [Do the letters make a long *e* sound?]

3. The *(cashiers, casheirs)* at that grocery store are always friendly.

4. We're taking care of my *(nieghbors', neighbors')* dog while they are on vacation.

5. Do all lawyers carry a *(breifcase, briefcase)*?

GO ON

6. Listening to the soothing sounds of the ocean, we sat on the *(peir, pier)* for hours.

7. How many *(pieces, peices)* does that jigsaw puzzle have?

8. What a beautiful *(veiw, view)* you have from this window!

9. Several members of the soccer team were ill, so they had to *(forfiet, forfeit)* the game.

10. According to ancient *(beliefs, beleifs)*, Earth was at the center of the universe.

TIP Because there are so many exceptions to spelling rules, it is always a good idea to use a dictionary if you are not sure how to spell a word.

EXERCISE B   Underline the word in parentheses that is spelled correctly in each of the following sentences.

Examples 1. Look at all those wildflowers blooming in the (<u>field</u>, feild). [The letters make a long *e* sound, but they do not follow *c*. The correct spelling is *field*.]

    2. I can't wait to put these glow-in-the-dark stars on my (<u>ceiling</u>, cieling)! [The letters make a long *e* sound, and they follow *c*. The correct spelling is *ceiling*.]

11. Our high school band *(achieved, acheived)* their goal when they placed first in the state marching band contest. [Do the letters make a long *e* sound? Do they immediately follow *c*?]

12. Are you taking German or Spanish as your *(foreign, foriegn)* language? [Do the letters make a long *e* sound?]

13. If blood is red, why do our *(viens, veins)* look blue?

14. Cartoon characters often get into a lot of *(mischief, mischeif)*.

15. My mom and I lift *(wieghts, weights)* three times a week.

16. Mr. Gomez asked me to give a *(brief, breif)* report about the fund-raiser.

17. Have you *(received, recieved)* the package I sent you?

18. *(Their, Thier)* yard is always well maintained.

19. Our science project is due on Friday, I *(beleive, believe)*.

20. I'd like to return this sweater, but I don't have the *(reciept, receipt)*.

Prefixes and Suffixes

Prefixes

A prefix is a letter or group of letters added to the beginning of a word to change its meaning.

16e. When a prefix is added to a word, the spelling of the original word remains the same.

> **EXAMPLES** im + print = im**print**   pre + test = pre**test**

EXERCISE A Add the prefix to the word for each of the following items.

Example 1. co + operate = _____*cooperate*_____ [Adding the prefix *co*– does not change the spelling of *operate*.]

1. pre + view   = _____ [Does adding a prefix change the spelling of *view*?]

2. un + eventful = _____

3. im + patient   = _____

4. mis + understand = _____

5. re + organize   = _____

Suffixes

A suffix is a letter or group of letters added to the end of a word to change its meaning.

16g. Drop the final silent *e* before adding a suffix that begins with a vowel.

A silent *e* is not pronounced when you say the word.

> **EXAMPLES** celebrate + ation = **celebrat**ion   fine + est = **fin**est

TIP *Vowels* are the letters *a, e, i, o, u,* and sometimes *y*. *Consonants* are all the other letters.

16h. Keep the final silent *e* when adding a suffix that begins with a consonant.

> **EXAMPLES** waste + ful = **waste**ful   like + ly = **like**ly

EXERCISE B Add the suffix to the word for each of the following items.

Example 1. erase + ed = _____*erased*_____ [The suffix begins with a vowel, so the final silent *e* is dropped.]

6. blue + ish   = _____ [Does the suffix begin with a vowel or a consonant?]

7. time + less = _____

8. age + ing   = _____

9. peace + ful   = _____

10. bake + ed   = _____

GO ON ➡

16i. When a word ends in *y* preceded by a consonant, change the *y* to *i* before any suffix except one beginning with *i*.

EXAMPLES worry + ed = worr**ied**   worry + ing = worr**ying**

16j. When a word ends in *y* preceded by a vowel, simply add the suffix.

EXAMPLES display + ing = displ**aying**   buy + er = b**uyer**

EXERCISE C Underline the correct spelling of the combined word and suffix.

Example 1. tiny + er =   **a.** tinyer   **b.** tinier [Because *tiny* ends in a *y* preceded by a consonant, the *y* is changed to an *i* before the suffix is added.]

11. enjoy + ment =   **a.** enjoyment   **b.** enjoiment [When a word ends in a *y* preceded by a vowel, does the *y* change to *i* before adding the suffix?]

12. lonely + ness =   **a.** lonelyness   **b.** loneliness

13. rely + able =   **a.** relyable   **b.** reliable

14. say + ing   **a.** saying   **b.** saiing

15. likely + hood =   **a.** likelyhood   **b.** likelihood

16k. When a word ends in a consonant, double the final consonant before a suffix that begins with a vowel only if the word (a) has only one syllable or is accented on the last syllable and (b) ends in a single consonant preceded by a single vowel.

EXAMPLES run + ing = ru**nning**   prefer + ed = prefe**rred**

Otherwise, simply add the suffix.

EXAMPLES gift + ed = gift**ed**   direct + ion = direc**tion**

EXERCISE D Add the suffix to the word for each of the following items. Write the new word on the line provided.

Example 1. sit + ing = _____*sitting*_____ [The word has only one syllable and ends in a single consonant preceded by a single vowel. The correct spelling is *sitting*.]

16. begin + ing = _____ [Is the word accented on the last syllable? Does it end in a single consonant preceded by a single vowel?]

17. regret + able = _____

18. keep + er = _____

19. top + ed = _____

20. dent + ed = _____

Plurals of Nouns

Most nouns can be made plural simply by adding –s to the end of the word.

SINGULAR	apple	calendar	freeway	rodeo
PLURAL	apple**s**	calendar**s**	freeway**s**	rodeo**s**

Some nouns are made plural by adding –es to the end of the word.

SINGULAR	pitch	Lopez	box	hero
PLURAL	pitch**es**	Lopez**es**	box**es**	hero**es**

TIP▶ If the plural form of a word has one more syllable than the singular word has, the plural word is probably spelled with –es. A syllable is a word part that can be pronounced as one uninterrupted sound.

> **EXAMPLE**   The singular word *pitch* has one syllable. The plural word *pitches* has two syllables: *pitch•es*. The plural word *pitches* is formed by adding –es to the singular word *pitch*.

EXERCISE A Complete each sentence by writing the plural form of the boldfaced word on the line provided.

Examples 1. Eva grew up in a home full of ticking _____clocks_____. **clock** [The plural *clocks* has the same number of syllables as the singular *clock*. The plural is formed by adding –s.]

2. The courthouse museum is full of old wagon _____hitches_____. **hitch** [The plural *hitches* has one more syllable than the singular *hitch*. The plural is formed by adding –es.]

1. How many _____ are aboard this train? **passenger** [Does the plural form have the same number of syllables as the singular or does the plural form have one more syllable?]

2. How many _____ do you think we'll need for the move? **box** [Does the plural form have the same number of syllables as the singular or does the plural form have one more syllable?]

3. I always wash the _____ after dinner. **dish**

4. When she visited them, the _____ took Florence on a tour of the town. **Jordan**

5. I built a birdhouse, and now a family of _____ has a made a nest in it. **finch**

6. Wow, look at all those _____ hanging behind your computer! **cable**

7. Don't forget to water the _____. **flower**

8. The _____ in front of the school need to be painted. **bench**

9. After six or seven _____ we rolled out of the station. **lurch**

10. Have we received any _____ today? **fax**

GO ON ▶

Developmental Language Skills   **149**

Many nouns that end in –*y* form the plural by changing the *y* to *i* before adding –*es*.

| **SINGULAR** | dragonfly | trophy | lady |
| **PLURAL** | dragonfl**ies** | troph**ies** | lad**ies** |

The plurals of some nouns are formed in different ways. A few nouns do not change at all to form the plural.

| **SINGULAR** | mouse | knife | deer |
| **PLURAL** | mice | knives | deer |

EXERCISE B On the line provided, write the plural form of each of the following words.

Examples 1. cry _____cries_____ [The *y* in *cry* changes to *i* and –*es* is added to form the plural.]

2. spacecraft _____spacecraft_____ [The plural form of *spacecraft* does not change.]

11. woman _____ [Do any letters in *woman* change to form the plural?]

12. enemy _____ [Do any letters in *enemy* change to form the plural?]

13. self _____

14. moose _____

15. tragedy _____

16. thief _____

17. ally _____

18. wolf _____

19. child _____

20. shelf _____

To form the plural of numerals, letters, symbols, and words used as words, add an apostrophe and an *s*.

EXAMPLES How many *however*'s did I use in my essay?
My little brother has a hard time writing *5*'s.

EXERCISE C On the line provided, write the plural form of each of the following numerals, letters, symbols, and words used as words.

Example 1. *A* _____A's_____ [The plural of a capital letter is formed by adding an apostrophe and an *s*.]

21. *&* _____ [What is added to a symbol to make it plural?]

22. *17* _____

23. *i* _____

24. *that* _____

25. *$* _____

Third Course

Words Often Confused A

People often confuse the following words. Some of these words are *homonyms*—that is, their pronunciations are the same. However, these words have different meanings and spellings. Other words in the following groups have the same or similar spellings yet have different meanings.

affect   [verb] *to influence*
This film will **affect** everyone in the audience.

effect   [noun] *result, consequence*
List two **effects** of good study habits.
[verb] *to bring about, to accomplish*
The committee **effected** the suggested changes.

all ready   [adjective] *everyone or everything prepared*
Are we **all ready** to load the van?

already   [adverb] *previously*
They're **already** inside.

all together   [adjective or adverb] *everyone or everything together in the same place*
Is everything **all together** and ready to go?

altogether   [adverb] *entirely*
This seems **altogether** too simple.

EXERCISE A Underline the word or words in parentheses that will complete the sentence correctly.

Examples 1. Aunt Nina said that she was (*all together,* <u>*altogether*</u>) pleased by the thoughtful gift.
[The meaning is "entirely," so *altogether* is correct.]

2. What is the (*affect,* <u>*effect*</u>) of sprinkling salt on ice? [The meaning is "result," so *effect* is correct.]

1. Please don't use those neon posterboards; they're (*altogether, all together*) too bright. [Which word means "entirely"?]

2. Dad said the boxes are packed and are (*already, all ready*) to be loaded on the truck. [Which words mean "everything prepared"?]

3. One (*affect, effect*) of an increase in rainfall is thickened undergrowth.

4. Have you (*all ready, already*) fed the cats?

5. We were (*all ready, already*) for the grand opening of the new community center.

6. Mrs. Finley's math class met (*already, all ready*).

7. How do colors (*effect, affect*) our emotional state?

Developmental Language Skills

8. The ducks are *(all together, altogether)* on the shore of the pond.

9. Do commercials *(effect, affect)* your decision to buy certain products?

10. We met in the lobby and went into the ballroom *(all together, altogether)*.

---

brake   [noun] *a stopping device*
Pulling this lever will apply the **brake.**
[verb] *to stop*
This time, try to **brake** before we reach the curb.

break   [verb] *to shatter, sever*
The sign read, "If you **break** it, you buy it."

choose   [verb, present tense, rhymes with *shoes*] *select*
Which puppy did you **choose?**

chose   [verb, past tense, rhymes with *nose*] *selected*
I **chose** this one.

EXERCISE B Underline the word in parentheses that will complete the sentence correctly.

Examples 1. I'm glad that the vase didn't <u>(break</u>, brake) when I dropped it. [The meaning is "to

shatter," so *break* is correct.]

     2. It usually takes me forever to <u>(choose</u>, chose) a birthday card. [The meaning is "select,"

so *choose* is correct.]

11. Mary *(choose, chose)* to do her science report on NASA's Mars Exploration Program. [Which

word means "selected"?]

12. How long does it take a car to stop after you apply the *(brakes, breaks)*? [Which word means "a

stopping device"?]

13. Whom did Coach Ramirez *(choose, chose)* for the starting lineup?

14. This coconut refuses to *(brake, break)* open!

15. Since it's your birthday, you get to *(choose, chose)* the restaurant and the movie.

16. Have you ever seen the bumper sticker that says, "I *(break, brake)* for garage sales"?

17. My uncle *(breaks, brakes)* different kinds of tile and glass to make mosaics.

18. What types of material does a bird *(chose, choose)* when it wants to make a nest?

19. Always check your *(brakes, breaks)* after you drive through water.

20. Last year we *(chose, choose)* to plant herbs rather than flowers in the window box.

Words Often Confused B

People often confuse the following words. Some of these words are *homonyms*—that is, their pronunciations are the same. However, these words have different meanings and spellings. Other words in the following groups have the same or similar spellings yet have different meanings.

coarse   [adjective] *rough, crude*
The surface of this tree's bark is fairly **coarse.**

course   [noun] *path of action or progress; unit of study; track or way; part of meal*
The jogger's **course** will cross the park.
Try taking a **course** in music appreciation.
[also used with *of* to mean *naturally* or *certainly*]
Of **course,** I'll be at your recital.

desert   [noun, pronounced des'•ert] *a dry region*
It's as dry as a **desert** in here.

desert   [verb, pronounced de•sert'] *to leave*
Soldiers never **desert** their posts.

dessert   [noun, pronounced de•sert'] *a sweet, final course of a meal*
Why can't we eat **dessert** before the meal?

hear   [verb] *to receive sounds through the ears*
Can you **hear** me?

here   [adverb] *at this place*
Meet **here** at five o'clock.

EXERCISE A Underline the word in parentheses that will complete the sentence correctly.

Examples 1. That fabric is too (*coarse, course*) to use for a pillowcase. [The meaning is "rough," so *coarse* is correct.]

        2. Wasn't that (*dessert, desert*) tasty? [The meaning is "a sweet, final course of a meal," so *dessert* is correct.]

1. (*Hear, Here*) are the supplies you requested. [Which word means "at this place"?]

2. Kangaroo rats live in the (*desserts, deserts*) of North America. [Which word means "a dry region"?]

3. I don't really like sweets, so I usually eat some fruit for (*dessert, desert*).

4. Over the (*course, coarse*) of the summer, I ran a total of two hundred miles.

5. The rock's texture is very (*course, coarse*).

6. Eagles don't (*desert, dessert*) the nests they build; they use the same nest each year.

Developmental Language Skills

7. Which golf *(course, coarse)* is the most challenging?

8. Please bring those flowers over *(hear, here)*.

9. Should I take the creative writing *(coarse, course)* this semester or next semester?

10. Dogs certainly *(hear, here)* well.

---

its   [possessive of *it*] *belonging to it*
The nest and **its** lining of feathers keep the bird dry.

it's   [contraction of *it is* or *it has*]
Don't tell Ramona about the party; **it's** a surprise.
It's been an exciting week!

lead   [verb, present tense, rhymes with *deed*] *to go first*
You should **lead** us in the first chorus.

led   [verb, past tense of *lead*, rhymes with *fed*] *went first*
He **led** them over rough terrain.

lead   [noun, rhymes with *red*] *a heavy metal; graphite in a pencil*
This suitcase is as heavy as **lead.**
I need to sharpen the **lead** of my pencil.

EXERCISE B Underline the word in parentheses that will complete the sentence correctly.

Examples 1. The drum major *(lead, led)* the band across the field. [The meaning is "went first," so *led* is correct.]

2. Why does your dog chase *(its, it's)* tail? [The meaning is "belonging to it," so *its* is correct.]

11. Which float will *(lead, led)* the parade? [Which word means "to go first"?]

12. This jacket is missing three of *(its, it's)* buttons. [Which word means "belonging to it"?]

13. Do you know if *(it's, its)* supposed to rain this weekend?

14. These tracks in the sand tell us that one coyote *(led, lead)* the others.

15. The snake is shedding *(its, it's)* skin.

16. Hurry, *(its, it's)* almost time for the movie to start!

17. Coach Quadri *(lead, led)* the team to another successful season.

18. Much *(lead, led)* is recovered from recycled scrap.

19. Mr. Simmons will *(lead, led)* you through the museum and answer any questions you may have.

20. I need some more *(led, lead)* for my mechanical pencil.

Words Often Confused C

People often confuse the following words. Some of these words are *homonyms*—that is, their pronunciations are the same. However, these words have different meanings and spellings. Other words in the following groups have the same or similar spellings yet have different meanings.

passed [verb, past tense of *pass*] *went by*
We already **passed** that sign an hour ago.

past [noun] *history, what has gone by*
People can learn from what happened in the **past.**
[adjective] *former*
Don't dwell on **past** troubles.
[preposition] *farther than; after*
He threw the ball **past** the foul line.

peace [noun] *absence of conflict*
This treaty will ensure a lasting **peace** in the region.

piece [noun] *a part of something*
This is the last **piece** of the puzzle.
[verb] *to assemble slowly*
First, we will **piece** the quilt together.

quiet [adjective] *silent, still*
Her voice was almost too **quiet** to hear.

quite [adverb] *to a great extent or degree, completely*
This was **quite** an easy task.

EXERCISE A Underline the word in parentheses that will complete the sentence correctly.

Example 1. The thunder was (*quiet, quite*) loud. [The meaning is "to a great extent," so *quite* is correct.]

1. This single (*peace, piece*) of hardware will double the speed of your system. [Which word means "a part of something"?]

2. I feel at (*peace, piece*) when I'm surrounded by my family.

3. By the time the speaker reached the podium, the audience was (*quiet, quite*).

4. In the (*passed, past*), geese have nested here.

5. Little time has (*past, passed*) since we sat down.

GO ON

their [possessive of *they*] *belonging to them*
These are **their** favorite photographs.

there [adverb] *at that place*
You left your shoes over **there.**
[also used to begin a sentence]
There is a boat ramp at Browne Park.

they're [contraction of *they are*]
I know that **they're** under the sofa.

to [preposition; also used before infinitive form of a verb]
We should go **to** the store.
I'm going **to** sing like a whale.

too [adverb] *also; excessively*
I saw that game, **too.**
The film was **too** short.

two [adjective or noun] *the sum of one + one*
There are only **two** doors to this car.

EXERCISE B Underline the word in parentheses that will complete the sentence correctly.

Examples 1. They should be proud of (*their*, *they're*) achievements. [The meaning is "belonging to them," so *their* is correct.]

 2. When you go (*too*, *to*) the store, buy some fresh flowers. [*To* is a preposition that helps identify where you went.]

6. Did David call, (*two*, *too*)? [Which word means "also"?]

7. (*There*, *Their*) is more than one correct answer to some questions. [Which word is used to begin a sentence?]

8. In (*two*, *too*) days, the pool will open!

9. Sharon wants (*to*, *too*) be a firefighter.

10. Do you want me to set this box over (*their*, *there*) by the window?

11. My cats love (*to*, *two*) catch bugs.

12. (*Their*, *They're*) planning a surprise party for Jill's birthday.

13. Is this picture frame (*too*, *two*) big?

14. This is (*there*, *their*) first trip to New York.

15. The filing cabinets are (*too*, *to*) heavy to move when they're full.

Common Errors Review

Common Usage Errors

Be sure to proofread each writing assignment before you turn it in. Errors in writing can confuse and distract readers, and careless mistakes may even lead readers to form poor impressions of a writer. Look for errors by asking yourself these questions:

Are subjects and verbs in agreement?   Are modifiers correct and placed correctly?
Are verb tenses and forms correct?   Are troublesome words correct?
Are pronoun references clear?   Is usage appropriate to audience and purpose?

After you make any corrections or changes to your writing, read your writing again. Sometimes a change you make will create the need to adjust another part of your writing.

The following exercises will help you recognize and correct common errors in usage and mechanics.

EXERCISE A Use the list of questions above to help you find and correct the common errors in usage found in the following sentences. Use proofreading marks to make your corrections.

Example 1. Every year, after the holidays is over, Sandra and Martin plan they're gardens. *(are; their)*

[*Holidays* is plural, so it should take the plural verb *are*. *They're* is a contraction of *they are*, while *their* is the correct possessive pronoun.]

1. Sandra and Martin built their first garden in Sandra's backyard, but it ran out of room, so they find a new plot in the city's garden area. [Does a neuter singular pronoun refer to the wrong antecedent? Is a verb in the wrong tense?]

2. Looking for new kinds of vegetable to grow, seed catalogs are read quickly by the two. [Does the sentence contain a singular noun that should be plural? Is there a misplaced modifier? Is there an independent clause in the passive voice?]

3. They try and raise new varieties every year, and they do all of the gardening themselves.

4. Her and Martin plant carrots, radishes, and lettuce early in the season.

5. During last spring's cooler weeks, Martin, for who tomatoes are a treat, bought tomato plants and stakes at a local nursery.

6. Sandra and him go to plant the tomatoes, but they found that they still had work to do.

7. Sprouting from the well-tilled soil, they found weeds, but neither teen would want to pull them.

GO ON

8. Luckily, two nearby gardeners said that they will help, if, once they finished weeding Sandra

and Martin's garden, Sandra and Martin was to help them in return.

9. Sandra and Martin, when their own garden finished, helped their new friends plant

vegetables for theirselves.

10. Martin and Sandra now garden very good, especially after having got so much practice.

Common Mechanics Errors

Be sure to check your capitalization, punctuation, and spelling when you write. Use a
dictionary if you're not sure of a spelling or of how to divide a word. Make sure you haven't
confused two words that sound alike but are spelled differently. Attention to these details will
make a big difference in your writing! Ask yourself these questions as you proofread your
work:

Does every sentence begin with a capital letter?
Are all proper nouns capitalized?
Does every sentence end with an appropriate end mark?
Are words spelled and divided correctly?
Have you placed commas and apostrophes where they are needed?
Are direct quotations and titles capitalized and punctuated correctly?

EXERCISE B Correct errors in capitalization, punctuation, and spelling in the following sentences. Use
proofreading marks to make your corrections.

Example 1. Wasn't surfing once banned in hawaii? [Proper nouns should be capitalized, and
questions should end with question marks.]

11. Some people beleive that Duke paoa kahanamoku the winner of three Olympic gold medals

was the world's best freestyle swimmer. [Is there a misspelled word in this sentence? Is there an

appositive phrase that needs to be set off with commas? Should any words be capitalized?]

12. He won gold medals in 100-meter freestyle events in stockholm (1912) and Antwerp (1920),

and he was a member of the winning United states team in the 800-meter relay.

13. Didnt he take his ten-foot surfboard with him whenever he traveled outside Hawaii!

14. "I am only happy, he once said, "When I am swimming like a fish."

15. He had a worldwide affect on the sport; by the time of Duke's death, surfing had become

quiet popular all over the world.